MW01291756

Paulo Freire

Paulo Freire

His Faith, Spirituality, and Theology

Foreword by Ana Maria Araújo Freire

James D. Kirylo
University of South Carolina, USA

and

Drick Boyd
Eastern University, USA

SENSE PUBLISHERS
ROTTERDAM/BOSTON/TAIPEI

A C.I.P. record for this book is available from the Library of Congress.

ISBN: 978-94-6351-054-7 (paperback)
ISBN: 978-94-6351-055-4 (hardback)
ISBN: 978-94-6351-056-1 (e-book)

Published by: Sense Publishers,
P.O. Box 21858,
3001 AW Rotterdam,
The Netherlands
https://www.sensepublishers.com/

All chapters in this book have undergone peer review.

Printed on acid-free paper

ADVANCE PRAISE FOR
PAULO FREIRE: HIS FAITH, SPIRITUALITY, AND THEOLOGY

"James D. Kirylo and Drick Boyd's powerful essays text on the faith, spirituality, and theology of Paulo Freire provide a unique and much needed contribution to our understanding of one of the most influential educational philosophers of the 20th century. By way of thoughtful engagement with Freire's lived history, praxis, and political sensibilities, they reintroduce us to the man from Recife, through his radical sense of hope, undaunted faith, and the beauty of his implicit spirituality."
– Antonia Darder, Leavey Endowed Chair of Ethics & Moral Leadership at Loyola Marymount University and Distinguished Visiting Professor at the University of Johannesburg

"Freirean orthopraxis has a redemptive as well as protagonistic role. To deny spirituality as part of Freire's pedagogy of liberation is to enable the abscess of reason to pacify what can only be understood as Freire's fundamental revelation: to take down from the cross all those who suffer from the crimes of the state. Thus, the generative power of Freire's pedagogy presents us with a formidable weapon for unmasking the structural sins of the state (i.e., economic inequality, racism, patriarchy) and for emboldening our commitment to justice for those whom democracy has disinherited: the poor and the powerless. Kirylo and Boyd have made an important contribution to our understanding of Freire and his work, and in so doing have taken us further down the long road to justice."
– Peter McLaren, Distinguished Professor in Critical Studies, Co-Director, The Paulo Freire Democratic Project and International Ambassador for Global Ethics and Social Justice, College of Education, Chapman University

"This book is indeed an invaluable read for anyone interested in exploring the often-overlooked spiritual dimension in the work of one of the most influential educators of the 20th century. Freire's pedagogy was deep-rooted and substantiated by his Christian faith, which provided him the inspiration to work relentlessly to denounce all systems of oppression that dehumanize people and steal their agency and to announce the sacredness of life which implies dignity for all. Drawing from a wide range of religious thinkers and leaders, James Kirylo and Drick Boyd skillfully interweave Freire's life, work, and spirituality offering us new lenses to see Freire's praxis as a result of his ethical commitment to the world and the people in their material and spiritual aspects."
– Débora B. Agra Junker, Founder and Director of the Cátedra Paulo Freire at Garrett-Evangelical Theological Seminary

*Be not conformed to this world: but be ye transformed
by the renewing of your mind.*

(Romans 12:2)

*The hope of a secure and livable world lies with disciplined
nonconformists, who are dedicated to justice, peace and
brotherhood. The trailblazers in human, academic, scientific
and religious freedom have always been nonconformists.
In any cause that concerns the progress of mankind,
put your faith in the nonconformist!*

(Martin Luther King, Jr.)

In the final analysis, the Word of God is inviting me to re-create the world, not for my brothers' [and sisters'] domination, but for their liberation.

(Paulo Freire)

TABLE OF CONTENTS

ANA MARIA ARAÚJO FREIRE

FOREWORD

There are moments in my life when a longing for the presence of Paulo and the pain of his loss bring forth, in a seemingly contradictory manner, an outpouring of true joy from me.

Such is happening at this moment: the happiness and the immense longing for Paulo take form in a task, which although difficult, is at the same time pleasurable because it brings him back to me.

What awakens this feeling in me was the invitation from James D. Kirylo and Drick Boyd to provide the foreword for the book that four hands, two souls, and two heads, united as if as a single being, wrote about my husband Paulo Freire.

The title, *Paulo Freire: His Faith, Spirituality, and Theology*, invokes our curiousity and encourages us to read about a facet of Paulo, which in recent years has been ignored: his faith and his spirituality.

The search for this metaphysical side of Paulo, which was manifested in his acts, gestures, and practices, in his commiseration for and togetherness with the poor and those who suffered injustices, is, I believe, the life history of the authors. James had Catholic upbringings and almost became a priest. Drick describes his early work, some of the difficult challenges he faced as a youth worker, and his search for what his life would become leading to his becoming a Pastor. Today they have gone different ways. Both are teachers in the area of education concerned with religious development and social justice.

In the book, they narrate, analyze, formulate hypotheses, draw parallels, and contrast ideas of other authors with those of Paulo, and discuss the epistemological theory of the educator from Pernambuco with propriety, seriousness, and competence. And they delight and astonish us by their ability to simultaneously form a critical analysis, a deep search for the virtues of Paulo – demonstrated in his faith and spirituality, which forged a new theology, "wet", as Paulo himself put it, in the experience of his life and praxis – with the enormous capacity of the educator to observe, learn, verify, think, reflect, and create things: absolutely new practices and ideas, putting them on paper as political and loving acts. Fortunately, James and Drick lovingly understood the cognitive path that is guided by intelligence and the ability to tap into Paulo's thoughts as they demonstrate in their critical-comparative narrative of this excellent work.

The bibliography set down by the authors includes nearly all of Paulo's work, surely all published in the English language; the attraction that they sensed through the writings of a man who broke the most hidden, and at times, the most obvious soul and utopian dreams of human beings; the sense of goodness and solidarity of a man who lived for 75 years searching for truth, with tolerance, simplicity, coherence, and generosity, from his love for human beings (of any origin, age, religion, or sexual orientation) that impregnated his theory and his praxis toward the pursuit of this greatest dream: social justice, and as such, authentic democracy. I affirm with no tredipation that this profound work will become a classic in the literature of pedagogy and even in religious literature inlcuding the study of the philosophy of religions.

They point to the influences of humanism, personalism, and Marxism in Paulo, but stay true to my husband's originality of thought, to his composition of a theory of knowledge, which is not a junction of different theories, but is, to the contrary, an educational theory: political, ethical, with a philosophical basis, anthropological, and theological.

Paulo worked at the World Council of Churches for 10 years in Geneva at the position created especially for him, as an educator surrounded by the great theologians of Christian churches, not just Catholic, who taught him a great deal. But his faith in God, his "camaraderie" with Christ came from the Catholic upbringings of his mother, who made the choice to raise her four children in this way.

His ethical, scientific, and anthropological development were made possible by my parents, Aluizio and Genove Araújo, who provided him with a scholarship at the school they owned, the *Colégio Oswaldo Cruz*, in Recife in the 1940s where I met him. This school, known for its highest moral, civic, and scientical qualities, has graduated hundreds of young people from the *Nordeste*, the Northeast of Brazil.

Paulo's political development was, in fact, self developed. Born not only from his studies, but also from books of the most varied ideological strains, which, through his own lens, forged a political pedagogy centered on compassion and engagement with the "*esfarrapados*" or "ragged ones" of the world and within his praxis that included the oppressed classes and with those of different genders, religions, races or ethnicities.

Finally, I want to highlight the incisive perception of the authors about Paulo's dialectical understandings, particularly when they address *conscientização*, which arises from Paulo's political understandings and not, as it might seem to many, arising from his spirituality. I also want to emphasize the authors' understanding of the denunciation-announcement concept as a concomitant act and not, as viewed by positivist thinkers, as one that follows from the other. For Paulo, conscientious and critical denunciation brings at its core the announcement of the new. Denunciation of the ugly and that which is evil is an act that also simultaneously announces the dreamed dream, the hope for a better future.

I conclude my words inviting potential readers and actual readers of this work to establish with James and Drick a loving dialogue comparable to how they established their own dialogue with Paulo seeking out the roots of things and the substantivity of phenomena.

I can without fear assure that much will be learned by the reader from all three: a European-born, James; a North American, Drick; and a Brazilian from the "*terras quentes*" and refreshing breezes of the *Nordeste*, from Recife, the beloved city of my unforgettable husband Paulo who, through his genius and humility, illuminated the making of this book.

Thank you so much, James and Drick, for inviting me to be a part of this book, which brings the presence of the man from Recife who became a man of the world, Paulo Freire.

Nita
Jaboatão dos Guararapes, at the end of the
afternoon of May 23, 2017

ACKNOWLEDGEMENTS

The process of writing this book was an enriching experience, enabling us to individually know deeper the spiritual foundation that profoundly framed the philosophy that guided Paulo Freire's activism, ultimately inspiring us even more to continue the work of justice, equity, and the furthering of humanizing humanity.

Engaging in this project could not have been completed without the support and assistance of several people, who, with great gratitude, we would like to pay tribute. Many thanks to Ana Maria (Nita) Araújo Freire, Paulo's widow, who despite her ever-present busy schedule, took the time to write the Foreword to this book. We are honored. Thank you Edwin Dickey for translating Nita's Foreword, nicely capturing her thought from Brazilian Portuguese to English.

A million thanks to our esteemed colleagues Peter McLaren, Antonia Darder, and Débora Junker for taking the time to write respective praises for this work. We are humbled with your words of support for this important project.

Thank you, Jerry Aldridge and Kathy Hastings for their insightful, timely critiques, and much appreciation to Kathleen Duffy whose research informed us about the New Sanctuary Movement, all of which greatly added to the richness of this text.

David Armand your editorial assistance is greatly appreciated. In addition, thanks for our respective graduate assistants, Christopher Khaleel (as in the case of James) and Arlicia Etienne (as in the case of Drick), both of whom were helpful in moving this project along with checking references, finding articles, and other related research assistance.

Thank you, Michel Lokhorst, Publishing Director, at SENSE. Much appreciation for you believing in this project! And many thanks, Jolanda Karada, Production Coordinator at SENSE who once again has been a pleasure to work with to bring this book to final publication!

Finally, I (James) would deeply like to thank the three most important persons in my life. To Anette, my wife, who has always been supportive of my work, for which I am eternally grateful. And for our two boys, Antonio and Alexander. As they grow older, our hope is that they will come to deeply learn the greatness of Paulo Freire, and to be greatly influenced by his thought and spirituality. And I (Drick) thank my wife, Cynthia, for her quiet support. I also am grateful to my colleagues in POWER (Philadelphians Organized to Witness Empower and Rebuild) who everyday witness to their faith through their commitment to social justice.

INTRODUCTION

Paulo was a man of authentic faith that believed in God. And while he was Catholic, he was not caught up in the "religiosity" of the faith. He believed in Jesus Christ, and in His kindness, wisdom, and goodness.

(Freire, 2011, p. 278)

The Hispanic-Latinx Center at Garrett-Evangelical Theological Seminary in Illinois honored Paulo Freire with the naming of *Cátedra* Paulo Freire in April, 2016.[1] A Spanish-Portuguese term, *Cátedra* comes from the Latin word cathedra (chair), which originates from the Greek word for seat, possessing two broad meanings.

On one hand, in Roman Catholicism, for example, one who literally sits in the cathedra (or throne) is the bishop at a cathedral setting. On the other hand, in an academic setting, the person who "sits" on the cathedra is one who is honored for his/her outstanding contributions to a particular discipline, worthy to be remembered in the life-long preservation, studying, and investigation of that body of work.

Freire's recognition is, of course, related to the latter. In fact, the *Cátedra* Paulo Freire was the first Cátedra of its kind dedicated to Freire in the United States, particularly underscoring his contribution to theological and religious studies (http://catedra.garrett.edu/).[2,3]

This high honor that the Hispanic-Latinx Center at Garrett-Evangelical Theological Seminary bestowed on Paulo Freire is no small matter. It is indeed a public recognition that Freire possessed a certain spirituality that guided his thinking and work, so much so that this spirituality had an impact on theological and religious circles.

Freire, however, is more popularly recognized for his work in education, and is often referred to as the "father" of critical pedagogy and popular education, and is known worldwide as one of the most significant educational thinkers of the 20th century. Particularly illuminated with his seminal masterpiece, *Pedagogy of the Oppressed*, and later with other popular and highly influential works,[4] concepts related to banking/problem-posing education, dialogue, conscientização (conscientization), and justice are Freirean themes laced throughout his entire body of work. Moreover, those who have studied Freire's life and work speak of the radical social, educational, and political nature of his thought, and his lifelong commitment to education as a means to human liberation.

What is less known about Freire, but equally important, is the influence of his Christian faith on his overall educational philosophy and vision. Obviously, as resoundingly affirmed by the *Cátedra* Paulo Freire, Freire was a man who reflectively filtered his thought through a spiritual lens so much so that his work was also influential outside the circle of education, as it were.

Students of Freire familiar with theological terminology can sense a resemblance in his writing to the language and spirit of theological thinking. Throughout his work he uses words like love, hope, faith, Easter, conversion, and other related concepts, all of which carry religious or spiritual connotations. While there are only a few works in which Freire explicitly writes and speaks about his religious beliefs, those writings, nevertheless, are enough in making clear that there was a spiritual dimension to his thinking that had a profound influence on him.

There are, of course, a handful of scholars who have noted the spiritual dimension in Freire's thought. For example, Goodwin's *Reflections on Education* (1978) contrasts the educational strategies of Martin Luther King Jr., Paulo Freire and Jesus of Nazareth. While not minimizing the divinity of Christ, Goodwin's objective was to compare these three towering figures as "social educators," by connecting Freire with both King and Jesus, implying that Freire's thinking also has spiritual and theological significance.

John Elias, author of the influential book, *Paulo Freire: Pedagogue of Liberation* (1994) is one of the first to write extensively on the religious dimension of Freire's work, and also believes that since its publication in English, *Pedagogy of the Oppressed*, has been used by religious and theological thinkers more than any other discipline.[5] Fenwick and English (2004) go so far as to claim that Freire "saw his work as spiritual" (p. 51). Fraser (1997) interestingly puts it this way, "In other times and traditions, Paulo Freire would be seen as not only a great teacher but also a spiritual guide" (p. 175).

In addition to the above, several scholars have noted the connections between the writings of Freire and liberation theology (Aronowitz, 1998; Giroux, 1985; McLaren, 2000; Kirylo, 2011) and moreover many religious thinkers have drawn insights from his work (Goodwin, 1978; Gutiérrez, 1971; Schipani, 1984). Welton (1993) has even explored the parallels between Freire's concept of conscientization and the Christian concept of conversion.

PURPOSE OF BOOK

And while noted above, Freire wrote a handful of theological essays, often spoke to groups of religious educators and carried on meaningful dialogues with theological thinkers, the spiritual orientation guiding his thought and action is still relatively unexplored, and deserving of further examination.[6] In large part with respect to the latter, this is due to the fact that Freire infrequently referred to his "faith" (his word for his spirituality). Moreover, he admitted he was hesitant to speak about his faith, and so only did sparingly (Freire, 1992).

Until recently many scholars outside the theological disciplines were hesitant to speak of spirituality out of what Keating (2008) calls a "spirit phobia." In recent years, however, conversations on spirituality have expanded its traditional borders, and have become broader and more eclectic; that is, the concept of spirituality is becoming largely separated from simply a synonym for religious convictions. As

Ngunjiri (2011) has pointed out, spirituality is now openly discussed in disciplines as diverse as leadership, social work, education and nursing. In short, while religion and spirituality have an obvious connection to each other, in recent times it has come to be seen that the former does not contain or define the latter.[7]

To that end, the purpose of this volume aims to explore the connection between Freire's faith (as earlier mentioned, Freire's preferred term, rather than spirituality) and its impact on his thought, practice, and his overall work of fostering the humanization of humanity. While the sources of this book will be primarily drawn from Freire's work, secondary sources will be pulled from those who knew Freire, have written about him, and have been meaningfully impacted by him.

OVERVIEW OF CHAPTERS

In Chapter 1, *Spirituality and Paulo Freire*, the concepts of spirituality, religion, theology, and faith will be explored. While there is certain interrelatedness with these four concepts, they each possess distinct features about them that necessitates a conversation in order to establish working assumptions that framework this text. In Chapter 2, *The Easter Experience: Conversion to the People*, Freire's notion of faith and his concept of "conversion to the people" will be examined and its impact on the change of self and working toward making a more just and right world for all. *Personalism, Humanism, and a Freirean Spirituality Toward Humanizing Humanity*, the title of Chapter 3 clarifies the meaning of the philosophies of personalism and humanism and its influence on Freire's thinking and ultimately his spirituality. In Chapter 4, *Hope, History, and Utopia*, as the wording of the title indicates, are critical central themes in Freire's philosophy in the effort of being participatory subjects in the world. A common thread that weaved throughout Freire's life's work was the concept of love, which will be explored in Chapter 5, *Grounded in the Well of Love*, which makes a good transition to Chapter 6, *A Man who Humbly Lived in Authenticity*. There is no question that Freire was a humble man, and to live in humility requires one to appreciate what it means to live authentically.

Freire's concept of conscientization is one that is certainly critical to his thought, a dynamic that moves one from awareness to action, that is ongoing in the dialectical interweaving of thought and action, all of which is the theme for Chapter 7, *Conscientization: Inner and Outer Transformation for Liberation*. Chapter 8, *A Freirean Imprint on Liberation Theology*, as the title suggests, discusses Freire's critical influence on what is known as liberation theology. Finally, the *Epilogue, A Call to Reinvent*, brings all the chapters together, reflecting on the common threads that had been woven throughout all the chapters and the implications for the present day critical pedagogue.

While each chapter is, of course, unique unto itself, there is, however, from time to time, some natural intersectionality among chapters. For example, a detailed discussion on hope and utopia, as in Chapter 4 cannot be discussed without a nod to its link to love, and a more detailed discussion on love, as in Chapter 5, cannot be examined devoid of its association to the concept of hope. But such is the work of Paulo Freire, particularly highlighted in the interpretation of his notion of praxis in which intersects such concepts as love, faith, hope, conscientization, utopia, humility, unfinishedness, authenticity, and humanization. In other words, while each of the chapter themes and the associated concepts are unique unto themselves, and as we attempted to deconstruct them in the context of spirituality in seven separate chapters, it is only natural—because of the close association among the themes— that from time to time there may be some intersection or a critical reiteration from chapter to chapter.

IN BRIEF: OUR STORY

Whether one is doing curriculum work, writing a book, teaching, or conducting some kind of artistic creation, one's story is always intertwined in the work. Our lives are in a perpetual state of contextualization, in an ever-constant process of becoming, intersected with what we read, observe, the experiences we undergo, and the people we meet. In that light, therefore, in order to fully appreciate the motivation, purpose, and implications of this book, we think it would be helpful to provide a brief autobiographical account of our story.

The genesis of this book took place in 2014 when the both of us first met at the American Educational Research Association (AERA) conference in Philadelphia, PA, USA. Along with other contributors, we both were participating in a Paulo Freire Special Interest Group round table event, which naturally tapped into various Freirean themes. And one theme that particularly resonated with the both of us was concepts related to spirituality, theology, and faith. Indeed, Freire is widely recognized as one who has significantly contributed to the thinking of liberation theology. Subsequent to that 2014 conference, our conversation continued over the next few years with our shared admiration of Paulo Freire, his work, his thought and our mutual interest in social justice, the common good, and its intimate link to spirituality.

While we certainly have shared common interests and a certain shared spirituality, we are quite different from each other. I (James) have spent virtually my entire adult working life in education, 18 years teaching elementary school and the last near 20 years in higher education. The focus of my research has been related to critical pedagogy, spirituality (more specifically liberation theology), literacy, and teacher leadership.

I was born and raised in Europe, and grew up in the Roman Catholic tradition, at one time with one foot nearly entering into the seminary to study to become a Catholic priest. My spirituality—deeply linked to social justice and educational equality—is greatly influenced by a cross-section of people such as Jonathan Kozol, Henri Nouwen, Richard Rohr, Hélder Cámara, Therese of Lisieux ("The Little Flower"), Thomas Merton, James Cone, Gustavo Gutiérrez, Oscar Romero, Mother Teresa, Martin Luther King, Jr., Dietrich Bonhoeffer, and, of course, Paulo Freire, to name a few.

To that end, therefore, it is only natural that over the years the trajectory of my work has been filtered through a decidedly Christian spirituality, which is framed in the dialectical interweaving of reflective educational practice in the light of faith, with a core focus on the "least of these," or what the liberation theologian would characterize as making a preferential option for the poor. The aim of my faith, however, is not so much to proclaim what I believe, but rather to hopefully demonstrate in my life a sense of love and hope in which the Gospel message is illuminated. To put another way, it is attributed to Francis of Assisi for saying, "Preach the Gospel always, and if necessary, use words."

Indeed, when one carefully examines a critical cornerstone that filtered Paulo Freire's work, it was clearly influenced by the Gospel story—with an ecumenical spirit—in which love, faith, and hope was the foundation. My aim, our aim, in this text is to simply examine that cornerstone and its impact on Freire's thought and the implications for those of us who seek to make the world more loving, more kind, more human.

I (Drick) often tell people I have not had *a* career but rather a *series* of careers. Following graduation from college, I worked as youth worker in Boston, MA during the period when the city schools were being desegregated through a citywide busing effort ordered by Judge Arthur Garrity. Though the neighborhood I worked in (Jamaica Plain) was equally divided by Puerto Rican, African American and Irish Catholic families, with a small contingent of Cubans and Dominicans, the kids of various racial groups were bused across town to achieve racial balance in the schools. This decision was not well received by most communities, so when I arrived in the spring of 1975, violent outbreaks were occurring in neighborhoods across the city. In fact one weekend when the violence had risen to a fever pitch, my neighborhood was walled off by police barricades.

While still living and working in that neighborhood, I attended seminary where I first read Freire's *Pedagogy of the Oppressed*. I had become deeply enamored by liberation theology and the writings of Gustavo Gutiérrez, and so had the sense that Freire's insights could and should have an influence on my work as an aspiring Baptist pastor. However, there were few people who shared my interest in Freire's writings, and fewer still who could help me translate his words into action. So my interest in Freire remained strong but dormant during my sixteen years as a pastor in urban, small town and suburban churches.

In 1997 I left the pastorate and began teaching adult students returning to college to complete their undergraduate degrees. I eventually enrolled in a doctoral program focusing on adult education, where I again encountered Freire, along with Myles Horton, and the popular education movement. I employed Freire's dialogical approach to teaching and learning in my classes. I began to interact with other like-minded educators and was introduced to critical pedagogy, another area greatly influenced by Freire's writings. In 2007 I transferred from the adult education program to the Urban Studies program where I now teach courses in urban theology, racism, leadership and social justice.

During a sabbatical in 2011, I proceeded to read every writing by Freire in English I could get my hands on. For some time I had been curious about the theological concepts Freire often referred to in his work, and wrote an article on "The Critical Spirituality of Paulo Freire" (2012), which was positively received. I also wrote a white paper on popular education describing the ways in which popular education was being practiced by community educators in the U.S. and Canada. When James and I met at that AERA Conference in 2014, I saw an opportunity to explore more deeply my interest in Frere's spirituality, which led to our collaborative effort of this book.

Today, I am an active member of an urban Mennonite congregation actively involved in interfaith social justice efforts in our neighborhood, as well as across Philadelphia. I also have worked with community groups helping to develop grassroots leadership, and to address problems and challenges in their local communities. In my work as a professor, I introduce all my students to the writings of Freire, and many have found *Pedagogy of Oppressed* as life-transforming as I did years ago. Like James, my spirituality is not so much evidenced in what I believe or say, but rather in how I seek to live and work in relationship to the poor, the marginalized and disenfranchised of our society. As Jon Sobrino (1988) describes so clearly, my spirituality and my social justice efforts are integrally related to each other. My spirituality is in an ongoing process of what Freire calls "the Easter experience" as daily I seek to live into God's preferential option for the poor.

NOTES

1   Through the leadership of Freirean scholar, Dr. Débora Junker and others at Garrett-Evangelical Theological Seminary and with the blessings of Dr. Ana Maria (Nita) Araújo Freire, Paulo's widow, the reality of this event is indeed a dream especially realized by Dr. Junker.

2   http://catedra.garrett.edu/

3   At this particular event, Dr. Ana Maria (Nita) Araújo Freire gave two keynote addresses, one titled *Critical Pedagogy as an Act of Faith, Love and Courage*, and *The Legacy of Freire: Dreams and Challenges*. In addition, along with other esteemed presenters, long-time Freirean scholar, Daniel Schipani, lectured on *Freire's Contribution to Understanding and Fostering Healthy Spirituality*.

4   To name only a few of those works, see *Pedagogy of The Heart, Letters to Cristina: Reflections on my Life And Work, Pedagogy of Hope: Reliving Pedagogy of the Oppressed, Education for Critical Consciousness, Pedagogy of the City, The Politics of Education: Culture, Power, and Liberation, Teachers as Cultural Workers: Letters to Those Who Dare Teach, Pedagogy of Freedom: Ethics, Democracy, and Civic Courage*.

5   This assertion by Elias regarding the influential effect *Pedagogy of the Oppressed* on religious and theological thinkers was shared in a personal conversation with D. Boyd in 2011.

6   It is worth pointing out that about the same time of the publication of this book, Irwin Leopando's text, *A Pedagogy of Faith: The Theological Vision of Paulo Freire* (Bloomsbury, 2017), was also released.

7   While the concept of spirituality will be explored in Chapter 1, in brief, as a point of distinction between spirituality and religion, spirituality comes from the Latin *spiritus*, meaning "breath of life." It is a way of being and experiencing. Spirituality develops, as May (1953), Buber (1958), and others point out, through an awareness of a transcendent dimension and is distinguished by certain recognizable values in regard to self, others, nature, life, and whatever one views to be the supreme

or the ultimate. In contrast, religion can be defined as the social or organized means by which persons express spirituality (Grim, 1994). And while religion and spirituality can be interrelated, spirituality does not depend on religion. Spirituality exists without the structure of religion, but authentic religion cannot be without spirituality (Chandler, Holden, & Kolander, 1992).

REFERENCES

Aronowitz, S. (1998). Introduction. In P. Freire (Ed.), *Pedagogy of freedom: Democracy and civic courage* (pp. 1–19). Lanham, MD: Rowman & Littlefield Publishers, Inc.

Boyd, D. (2012). The critical spirituality of Paulo; Freire. *International Journal of Lifelong Education, 31*(6), 759–778.

Buber, M. (1958). *I and thou* (2nd ed.). New York, NY: Scribner.

Chandler, C. K., Holden, J. M., & Kolander, C. A. (1992). Counseling for spiritual wellness: Theory and practice. *Journal of Counseling and Development, 71*(2), 168–175.

Elias, J. L. (1994). *Paulo Freire: Pedagogue of liberation.* Malabar, FL: Kreiger Publishing Company.

Fenwick, T., & English, L. (2004). Dimensions of spirituality: A framework for adult educators. *Journal of Adult Theological Education, 1*(1), 49–64.

Fraser, J. (1997). Love and history in the work of Paulo Freire. In P. Freire, J. Fraser, D. Macedo, T. McKinnon, & W. Stokes (Eds.), *Mentoring the mentor* (pp. 175–200). New York, NY: Peter Lang.

Freire, A. M. (2011). An Interview with Ana Maria (Nita) Araújo Freire. In J. D. Kirylo (Ed.), *Paulo Freire: The man from Recife* (pp. 271–289). New York, NY: Peter Lang.

Freire, P. (1992). *Pedagogy of hope: Reliving the pedagogy of the oppressed.* New York, NY: Continuum.

Giroux, H. (1985). Introduction. In P. Freire (Ed.), *The politics of education* (pp. xi–xxvi). South Hadley, MA: Begin & Garvey.

Goodwin, B. (1978). *Reflections on education: A Christian scholar looks at King, Freire and Jesus as social and religious educators.* East Orange, NJ: Goodpatrick Publishers.

Grim, D. W. (1994). Therapist spiritual and religious values in psychotherapy. *Counseling and Values, 38,* 154.

Gutiérrez, G. (1971). *A theology of liberation.* Maryknoll, NY: Orbis Books.

Keating, A. (2008). I am a citizen of the universe: Gloria Anzaluda's spiritual activism as a catalyst for social change. *Feminist Studies, 34*(1–2), 53–70.

Kirylo, J. (2011). *Paulo Freire: The man from Recife.* New York, NY: Peter Lang.

May, R. (1953). *Man's search for himself.* New York, NY: Norton Publishers.

McLaren, P. (2000). *Che Guevara, Paulo Freire and the pedagogy of revolution.* Lanham, MD: Roman and Littlefield.

Ngunjiri, F. (2011). Studying spirituality and leadership: A personal journey. In H. Chang & D. Boyd (Eds.), *Spirituality in higher education: Autoethnographies* (pp. 183–198). Walnut Creek, CA: Left Coast Press.

Schipani, D. (1984). *Conscientization and creativity: Paulo Freire and Christian education.* Lanham, MD: University Press of America.

Welton, M. R. (1993). Seeing the light: Christian conversion and conscientization. In P. Jarvis & N. Walters (Eds.), *Adult education and theological interpretations.* Malabar, FL: Krieger Publishing.

SPIRITUALITY AND PAULO FREIRE

INTRODUCTION

Paulo Freire is considered one of the most influential educational thinkers in the twentieth century, the founder of popular education, and the inspiration for the field of critical pedagogy. Yet as Sternberg asserts "those of us who espouse critical pedagogy and embrace Paulo Freire's visions of praxis and conscientization work out of a tradition, often unknowingly, with deep ties to religious faith" (quoted in Neumann, 2011, pp. 609–610). While many have acknowledged his ties to liberation theology, his deep underlying faith out of which that theology arose is often overlooked. In fact for Freire his political radicalism was an expression of and an outgrowth of his deep spiritual connection to God (Neumann, 2011). The purpose of this chapter is to explore the various ways contemporary writers understand the concept of spirituality, and then to explore the manner in which Freire's spirituality aligns with these understandings, and then to explore the concrete ways he sought to live out his spiritual commitments.

WHAT IS SPIRITUALITY?

When speaking about his religiosity, Paulo Freire almost always referred to his "faith in Christ" or just "faith." In his era, the terms, faith, religion and spirituality were generally considered inter-related if not synonymous. In more recent years the term "spirituality" has taken on a more eclectic and all-encompassing meaning, where as "religion" refers to a formal set of beliefs and practices in and through which individuals live out their spirituality. However, spirituality has also come to refer to experiences and practices not necessarily tied to formal religious beliefs. Often one can hear people say they are "spiritual but not religious."

Beginning in the late 19th century, sociologists and psychologists such as Freud, Jung, Weber and Allport found the study of religion and spirituality (often referred to as religious experience) to be a rich area of research (Hill et al., 2000). These early thinkers largely concluded that religion and spirituality are significant dimensions of human experience that can either contribute to or detract from fruitful and healthy living. Historically, religion has helped individuals come to terms with the meaning of their lives, address questions of ultimate significance and connect individuals to their understanding of the Divine. However, as the assumed connection between religion and spirituality has increasingly been severed, religion has taken on an institutional flavor focused on the adherence to certain beliefs, liturgical practices, and codes of behavior, whereas spirituality has taken on a more individualized and personal focus having to do with one's beliefs and experiences with God, a higher power, or a transcendent sense of purpose. In this sense persons can consider themselves deeply spiritual even though they are not related to a particular religious institution or set of beliefs (Tisdell, 2003; Tolliver & Tisdell, 2006; Zwissler, 2007; Bellah, Madsen, Sullivan, Swidler, & Tipton, 1985).

Moreover, spirituality does not simply pertain to one's private beliefs, but can also reflect one's engagement in the public sphere; that is, spirituality can be private and public, individual and political. For many people spirituality is related to a belief in God, but for others it encompasses a commitment to the betterment of the human condition, preservation of the natural world, or the pursuit of values such as love, truth and peace. In this sense spirituality involves an awareness of the transcendent or sacred, and an outlook that makes one feel connected to something larger than themselves that informs their morals and actions. As such, spirituality nurtures one's commitment to issues of social justice and desire for social change. This type of spirituality is akin to liberation theology, which both influenced and was influenced by Paulo Freire, and goes so far as to assert that one's spirituality, by design, leads one to act for liberation of oneself and others (Gutiérrez, 2003; Bean, 2000; English & Gillen, 2000; Tisdell, 2000).

Fowler (1981) makes a distinction between religion, belief and faith that can be helpful here. Referring to the work of his mentor and colleague William Cantwell Smith, Fowler says that religion is "a cumulative tradition of various expressions of the faith of people in the past" (p. 9). Religion includes symbols, oral tradition, music, sacred texts, creeds, and other elements usually associated with religion. By contrast faith "is the person or group's way of responding to transcendent value and power" (p. 8). Whereas traditionally faith is practiced within a religious tradition, often people express faith without reference to a particular tradition or with reference to several traditions. Quoting Smith, he writes faith "is an orientation of the personality, to oneself, to one's neighbor, to the universe; a total response, a way of seeing whatever one sees and of handling whatever one handles....to see, to feel, to act in terms of a transcendent dimension (Smith, quoted in Fowler, p. 11). Faith is distinguished from belief in that belief is "the holding of certain ideas" and "arises out of the effort to translate experiences of and relation to transcendence into concepts or propositions" (p. 11). By contrast "Faith is the relation of trust and loyalty to the transcendent about which concepts or propositions – beliefs – are fashioned" (p. 11). What Fowler refers to as "faith" in this book we are using the term used in more contemporary settings: spirituality. When he referred to his ultimate trust in God, Freire used the word "faith;" we refer to it as his spirituality.[1]

In its most basic sense spirituality causes people to be more aware of their inner life, the persons around them and the general state of the world. When viewed this way, the ultimate goal of spirituality is to help people find personal meaning and become more fully human, while serving the purpose of improving the lives of those suffering in the world. One's sense of meaning may be found in God, through significant relationships, or in personal and social actions. At the same time, it must be recognized that one's spirituality always develops in a specific social and cultural context. Thus, it is important that we consider Freire's family life, his cultural context, his religious background and the socioeconomic forces that shaped his life (Tolliver & Tisdell, 2006; Keating, 2008; Gotz, 1997; Stanczak, 2006).

PAULO FREIRE'S FAMILY AND RELIGIOUS BACKGROUND[2]

Paulo Freire grew up in a time of personal and social struggle. Late in life he recalled the Brazil of his childhood as a place of great beauty but also a place of backwardness, misery, poverty, [and] hunger" (Freire, 1996, p. 15). While Brazil had freed itself from colonial rule, the mindset and structures of Brazil's colonial legacy persisted in the social structures. Brazilian society consisted of a small, but powerful wealthy elite, while masses suffered pervasive poverty. Born in 1921, as the youngest of four children, Freire's childhood years were shaped by the suffering caused by the global economic collapse following the 1929 stock market crash.

Freire grew up in a loving, middle class family with a father who worked as a military police officer and a stay-at-home mother. His earliest years were spent in a small house in the northeastern city of Recife. Freire particularly enjoyed the backyard of his home in which there was a lush mango tree under which he spent many joyful hours. However, when Paulo was three years old, his father had to retire from the police force due to debilitating arteriosclerosis. This began an extended period of downward mobility. His father tried to supplement his meager retirement pension by working at various jobs: carpentry, importing, and buying and selling fruit from the interior of the country.

When the Depression of the 1930s began to impact the family, they were forced to sell various items for cash as well as seek support from family members in order to make ends meet. As the effect of the Depression deepened, Freire experienced hunger, which he described as "a real and concrete hunger that had no specific date of departure [and which] arrives unannounced and unauthorized, making itself at home without an end in sight" (Freire, 1996, p. 15). Eventually, Freire's family lost the house because they could not pay the mortgage, forcing them to leave Recife. They moved to nearby Jaboatão, to a home that was smaller and more affordable, but enabled them to continue the appearance of a middle class existence. However, when he was 13 years old his father died, leaving Paulo and his family in a state of destitution. Paulo had to drop out of school for two years and experienced the stress of living a survival level of existence. The stress, hunger, and impoverishment of those years caused Freire to fall behind in school and to be diagnosed by some of his teachers as "mentally retarded." Consequently, he barely qualified for secondary school. He particularly struggled with spelling (which may have been an influence on his eventual interest in literacy work). Even so, through the support of his older siblings who were able to work and the ingenuity of his mother who got a job at a local private school, Paulo was eventually able to continue his education despite the increased hardship caused by his father's untimely death (Horton & Freire, 1990, pp. 23–27; Elias, 1994, p. 3; Jeria, 1986, pp. 9–11).

While deeply committed to each other and the welfare of their children, Freire's parents had distinctly different religious views. His father was a spiritualist. He believed in God but chose to not affiliate with any specific religious body or denomination. Instead he drew from a wide range of sources in nature, science, philosophy and theology to shape his religious beliefs. By contrast, Paulo's mother was a devout Roman Catholic, who in turn raised him in the faith and traditions of the Catholic Church (Kirylo, 2011). Later in life, Freire recalled being enamored with the rituals and sense of awe invoked by those rituals, even though he resisted the rigidity of the local priest's teaching (Freire, 1984). From his parents he learned two overriding values: consistency in treating all people equally regardless of their station in life, and respect for people of different viewpoints (Horton & Freire, 1990). Through those values he saw the importance of linking one's religious beliefs to positive action on behalf of others.

During adolescence, he abandoned his Roman Catholic faith, claiming he was "formed and deformed" by the Church (Freire, 1984). He related one incident where the priest tried to frighten his catechism students (of which Paulo was one) by talking about the eternal damnation and hell. Years later Freire wrote that he was deeply offended by that statement. However, in the next sentence he goes on to say he was struck by "the goodness, the strength to love without limits to which Christ witnessed" (Freire, 1984, p. 547). This same paradox of resistance to the formal rigidity of the Church but acceptance of Christ was reflected in a scene from a documentary made late in Freire's life. In one scene Freire leads the interviewer to the Catholic Church of his youth, and admits that he and the church did not always see eye to eye, but then says "me and Jesus, we are friends" (Stoney, 1996).

While in college, Freire was introduced to the Catholic personalist philosophies of Maritain, Bernanos and Mounier (Elias, 1994).[3] He also became involved with Catholic Action, a religious group that sought to live out its faith through actions of service toward others, especially the poor. Catholic Action was commissioned by the Church leaders to encourage "religiously approved behavior" among the laity (Horton & Freire, 1990; de Kadt, 1970).

FREIRE'S ADULT SPIRITUAL DEVELOPMENT

The chapter of Catholic Action in which Freire was involved was particularly concerned about the poverty conditions among the rural *campesinos*, who in essence were tenant farmers on lands owned by large and powerful landowners. Because the treatment of workers was largely unregulated by the Brazilian government, these workers were often exploited and oppressed by the landowners. In exchange for land and protection peasants were expected to remain loyal to the political views of their landowners, even as they were forced to live in subsistence conditions. Catholic Action organized peasants into *sindicatos*, or farmer's unions, that demanded better treatment and working conditions from their landowners. At the same time Catholic Action protested the incursion of United States corporations seeking to control land and resources in exchange for small returns to the Brazilian economy. They called for the nationalization of Brazilian industries and land reform as well. Because of these overtly political actions, Freire's chapter of Catholic Action was eventually shut down by the Roman Catholic hierarchy (Jeria, 1986). Thus began Freire's ongoing tension with the leadership of the Church, even as he embraced its essential teachings related to social justice.

These early experiences in Catholic Action led Freire to pursue his literacy work among the rural poor, and eventually led to his exile from Brazil. At the same time, during this period he developed lifelong friendships with individuals such as Dom Hélder Câmara and Camilo Torres, who became influential leaders in the liberation theology movement. Moreover, these experiences caused his spiritual sensitivities to become intricately and intimately related to a commitment to social change and a fight against oppression (Jeria, 1984).[4]

POPULAR EDUCATION AND EXILE

Freire's development as a popular educator occurred amidst tensions between conservative and progressive forces within the Roman Catholic Church on the one hand, and a rising interest across Brazil in literacy training throughout the country as a political strategy on the other. In 1947 upon graduating from law school, Freire went to work for the Servico Social da Industria (SESI) as the director of Education and Culture in his home state of Pernambuco helping families who were having difficulties implementing educational programs in their communities. In 1956 he was appointed to the head of Council on Education in Recife, the capital city of Pernambuco, and he became well known as an expert and advocate on literacy training across Brazil. He further developed his ideas about literacy training after helping found the Popular Culture Movement (MCP). By 1962 he was the extension services director at the University of Recife, and involved many college students in literacy programs around Recife and eventually throughout the states of northeast Brazil. His approach gained great praise for enabling illiterate peasants to learn how to read in 40 days well enough to pass the literacy test required of all registered voters (Kirkendall, 2004).

In 1961, Socialist Joao Goulart was elected president of Brazil. The United States government, still shaken by the Cuban Revolution and rise of Fidel Castro, took a cautious approach to Goulart. The US officials expressed concern about Goulart's leftist orientation and sought to moderate his views, as well as the views of many governors and mayors elected throughout Brazil, particularly in the northeast, by providing foreign aid with expectations of moderation tied to it. Freire's literary programs were one recipient of that aid. With President Goulart's enthusiastic support, Freire's literacy approach was being replicated in states and communities throughout Brazil, but particularly in the Northeast states. Goulart and his political allies saw Freire's methods, which included the raising of political consciousness, as beneficial to their progressive political causes. One Northeastern mayor referred to the program as "Revolution Through Education" (Kirkendall, 2004).

Meanwhile, progressive elements within the Roman Catholic Church had been challenging the church's longstanding alliance with political, economic and social elites, and had begun calling for the church to exercise a particular concern for the millions of urban and rural poor in the country, and to work for substantive social change. While many local priests working in poor parishes pushed these changes, the bishop of Recife, Dom Hélder Câmara, organized the National Council of Brazilian Bishops (CNBB) as an institutional voice working for these ends. Out of CNBB grew the Base Community movement, groups of peasants who came together to talk about how the practical implications of the liberating message of the Christian gospel could be applied in their communities. The base community movement drew much of its approach from Freire's literary work and its emphasis on "reading the world" and conscientization (de Kadt, 1970; Neuhouser, 1989).

However, reactionary and conservative forces within the Roman Catholic Church, the Brazilian political elite and the United States government became increasingly concerned that Brazil would go the way of Cuba, and seek to become politically and economically independent of the United States. In early 1964 the US Agency for International Development (AID) withdrew support for Freire's literacy program, and in March 1964 President Goulart, and a number of socialist governors and mayors were deposed by a military coup. At first the military leaders hesitated to arrest Freire in the regime change, but eventually he was relieved of his duties, and held in prison for 70 days. Meanwhile the Roman Catholic Church officials, some of whom were Freire's close associates, failed to come to his defense. Freire later said those 70 days transformed and radicalized his thinking on political matters. He eventually sought exile in Bolivia, and then settled in Chile, where he continued his work and began writing (deKadt, 1970; Kirkendall, 2004).

THE NATURE OF FREIRE'S SPIRITUALITY

In adulthood Freire clearly identified himself as a Christian, a "friend of Christ" and "a man of faith" (Elias, 1994; Freire, 2007; Horton & Freire, 1990). While he had an ongoing struggle with the Roman Catholic Church as an institution, some of his closest colleagues were clergy affiliated with Latin American liberation theology movement such as Gustavo Gutiérrez, Leonardo Boff, Frei Betto, and Dom Hélder Câmara (Jeria, 1986).

Freire rarely talked of God apart from God's relationship to persons in the context of history. He considered God a "presence in history," but believed it was human beings, not God, who made changes in the conditions of society (Freire, 1970). He believed that people needed to work to change their circumstances and could not simply wait on God to change people or their circumstances. God's role consisted of providing the vision of what human completeness and social justice looked like. Freire wrote, "[God's] transcendence over us is based on the fact of our knowledge of this finitude. For man [sic] is an incomplete being and the completion of his incompleteness is encountered in his relationship with his creator, a relationship which by its very nature … is always a relationship of liberation" (quoted in Elias, 1976b, p. 41). For Freire the purpose of both education and social justice work were to move toward this vision of completeness (Elias, 1976b).[5]

In perhaps his most succinct yet clear statement of faith, Freire wrote late in his life: "This is how I have always understood God – a presence in history that does not preclude me from making history, but rather pushes me toward world transformation, which makes it possible to restore the humanity of those who exploit and of the weak" (Freire, 1997, pp. 103–104.) Expanding on that perspective a bit more, he continued, "… the fundamental importance of my faith [is] in my struggle for overcoming oppressive reality and for building a less ugly society, one that is less evil and more humane" (Freire, 1997, p. 104). In these words, we see reflected the linkage between a concern for social justice with a spiritually inspired motivation, or what Keating (2008) refers to as "spirit activism."

When Freire began his literacy work, he did so motivated by his Christian faith (Elias, 1994). Yet, early in his career he explored how Marxist thought could inform his educational philosophy. This foray into Marxism impacted his view of faith. He described the impact this way:

> When I was a young man, I went to the people, to the workers, the peasants, motivated really, by my Christian faith … When I arrived with the people – the misery, the concreteness, you know! … The obstacles of this reality sent me – to Marx. I started reading and studying. It was beautiful because I found in Marx a lot of the things the people had told me – without being literate. Marx was a genius. But when I met Marx, I continued to meet Christ on the corners of the street – by meeting the people. (Elias, 1994, p. 42)

While many of his Roman Catholic contemporaries considered this link between Marx and Christ to be heretical, for Freire it was like fitting a hand into a glove. Marx provided him a view of history and the world through which he acted out the dictates of his Christian faith. Marx provided him a new way in which to encounter Christ – in the lives of the people with whom he was working. As Elias (1976a) contends, "As [Freire became] more Marxist, the religious inspiration of his social philosophy [became] more explicit" (p. 65).

This link between spirituality and social justice is further highlighted in Freire's comments about reading and responding to the Word of God. What Freire meant when he referred to the Word of God is not entirely clear, but at its heart the Word of God for him seemed to be the words of Christ recorded in the gospels (the books of Matthew, Mark, Luke and John in the New Testament). Speaking of the gospels, he wrote,

> I cannot know the Gospels if I take them simply as words that come to rest in me … On the contrary, I understand the Gospels, well or badly, to the degree I live them, well or badly. I experience them and in them experience

7

myself through my own social practice, in history with other human beings. (Freire, 1984, p. 548)

Just as all learning for Freire comes through the interplay of reflection and experience, so too he believed one could understand the directives of the Word of God only as one sought to live them out. Freire wrote: "I think that my attitude cannot be the attitude of an empty being waiting to be filled by the Word of God. I think also that in order to listen to it, it is necessary to be engaged in the process of the liberation of man [sic]" (quoted in Elias, 1976a, p. 64). For Freire this living out was not simply for one's personal edification and benefit, but to impact the world at large. He wrote, "In the final analysis, the Word of God is inviting me to re-create the world, not for my brothers' domination, but for their liberation" (Freire, 1972, p. 11).

When it came to prayer, Freire rejected the "magical thinking" that often characterized much religious practice among the poor. This kind of prayer only bound persons to their poverty to passively await for divine intervention, and played into the hands of the dominant elite that oppressed them (Freire, 1970). Instead, Freire believed that prayer should not excuse or ignore oppressive practices, and should ask God for strength and courage to overcome injustice. Speaking of his own attitude toward prayer, Freire (1997) said, "I have always prayed, asking that God give me increased disposition to fight against the abuses of the powerful against the oppressed." Speaking of his prayers for the oppressed, he wrote, "I have always prayed in order that the weakness of the offended would transform itself into the strength with which they would finally defeat the power of the great" (p. 65). By the same token, Freire was not one to ask God to bring about societal liberation, but rather saw that as the task of humanity to achieve. In other words, for Freire (1997), God projects the vision of how society should be, but it is the role of human beings to "make history" and bring about needed changes.[6]

Late in his life, Freire spoke openly about his spirituality in an interview with George Stoney (1996). Freire said "I think I am more a man of faith than a religious man… I strongly believe I would never not think of the existence of God for one second. Nevertheless, I don't feel too much a need for church … Because above all for me the true temple of God is your body, is my body, our bodies. Reflecting on his work Freire said, "I start from the world. Our great task is to make the heaven here and now, it is to build happiness here and not just wait before arriving there." Echoing his ongoing critique of the church, Freire said, "The church thinks just of heaven, but the goal is to make the heaven here and now." By contrast he embraced liberation theology which he said "does not dichotomize worldliness from transcendent reality."

Throughout the interview he referred to his friendship with Christ. At one point he said the following:

I am sure of the things we should ask ourselves every day is: Why am I here? Who am I? With whom do I fight? What is my dream? The more I ask questions like this, the more I conceive the need I have to be consistent with my friendship with Christ. Not fear of Christ, friendship with Christ. To be afraid of Christ is a way of offending and denying him, a contradiction. I cannot have Christ as a liberator of me and of us, if at the same time I am afraid of him. Maybe [I'm] afraid of offending him, but not afraid of him.

From these simple words in halting English, Freire clearly described a spirituality at the heart of his person and of his work, and a friendship with Christ that was central to his sense of being.

Freire adopted a form of what Michael Dantley (2003) calls a "critical spirituality." Dantley's critical spirituality brings together the insights of African American spirituality and critical theory, and is rooted in the Black church prophetic tradition. This prophetic tradition combines a deep sense of right and wrong with an outspoken resistance to oppression and a realistic pragmatism with what can be accomplished in the face of that oppression. Based in the Biblical story of the exodus of the Hebrew people from bondage under their Egyptian oppressors, critical spirituality reflects a perspective similar to that of liberation theologians. Like the liberation theologians, critical spirituality looks to Jesus as the friend of the oppressed and as one whose ministry and life point to the ultimate victory of justice over oppression (Boyd, 2012). Dantley sums up his critical spiritual perspective by saying one's spirituality "comes from one's internal belief that the *as is* of any given situation can be overcome for the better *not yet*" (Dantley, 2005a, p. 656, italics original).[7]

From his Latin American liberation theology perspective, Freire saw his faith as a source of motivation and hope in his work to overcome oppression and illiteracy. As we will see in the following chapters, he believed God provided a vision of a utopia, a preferred future of what could and should be, even as he felt called to become converted to the cause of the oppressed. His faith enabled him to resist and call out oppression through what he called denunciation, even as it also emboldened him to work for the vision of the future God called them to work toward.

CONCLUSION

Cornel West describes the great African American philosopher and sociologist W.E.B. Dubois as exhibiting "a self-styled spirituality that was not wedded to cognitive commitments to God talk." He goes on to say that Dubois was "religiously sensitive without being religious" (West & Buschendorf, 2016, p. 59). We believe much the same can be said of Paulo Freire. While he was shaped by religious and spiritual influences early in his life, and he was close friends with many religious thinkers, he did not think of himself as a religious or spiritual thinker. Yet, his commitment to combatting oppression and illiteracy, as well as his pedagogical philosophy, reflects an unmistakable spiritual foundation. Influenced by the eclectic spirituality of his father and the Roman Catholicism of his mother, Freire lived out worldly spirituality that recognized a transcendent cause and power beyond himself, even as he immersed himself fully in the world. He exhibited what Thomas Berry

9

calls a "public spirituality" characterized by "the functional values and their means of attainment in an identifiable human community" (Berry, 1990, p. 110).

NOTES

[1] While we are using the words "faith" and "spirituality" with a particular reference to God or a transcendent force beyond normal human experience, it can be noted for many people the word "faith" and increasingly "spirituality" are used without specific reference to a deity or transcendent being, but rather refer to a fundamental faith in the human family, which is revealed in how we related to each other. Purpel (1989) drawing from H. Richard Niebuhr's *Radical Monotheism and Western Culture* stresses that the value of faith is seen in the context of how people care, trust and relate to one another. Reinhold Niebuhr (1927) states succinctly "Men [and women] cannot create a society if they do not believe in each other" (p. 62). While stating this in an explicitly Christian theological framework, many non-theists would affirm the same sentiment.

[2] For the background of Freire's early life, we looked to Kirylo's work, *Paulo Freire: The Man from Recife* (2011).

[3] See Chapter 3 for a fuller explanation of Personalist philosophy.

[4] Sobrino, (1988) contends that spirituality and one's sense of the "holy" is directly related to one's commitment to and involvement with the poor. He writes, "I regard it as established that the practice of liberation prepares the ground for a basic spirituality" (p. 35). He goes on, "[The] de-centration of oneself, this transfer of one's ultimate concern from oneself to the life of the poor, … is the subjective experience of the holy" (p. 110). It is clear that for Freire his engagement with the poor in his literacy work enhanced his sense of God and motivated him even more fully.

[5] See Chapter 5 and the discussion of Freire's concept of unfinishedness.

[6] Freire differs somewhat from many liberation theologians when it comes to God's involvement in human history. Gutiérrez writes: "Human history, then is the location of our encounter with God" (1971, p. 189). When speaking of history, he meant that God encounters us in concrete historical events and places; the encounter with God must always be understood in context. Likewise, Sobrino (1988) insisted that all theology be "theologal" (pp. 71–73) meaning that persons and communities encounter God in concrete historical circumstances while at the same time recognizing God as transcendent and beyond history. This understanding of history led both Gutiérrez and Sobrino, along with most Latin American liberation theologians to believe that God was most profoundly and consistently encountered in one's relationship with and action on behalf of the poor.

[7] Jon Sobrino in *Spirituality of Liberation: Toward Political Holiness* (1988) echoes a similar sentiment when he writes "Spirituality is simply the spirit of a subject – an individual or a group – in its relationship to the whole of reality" (p. 13). Sobrino goes on to identify three perquisites of "genuine spirituality:" (1) an honest acknowledgement and engagement with reality, that is the way the world is, not as one wants it to be; (2) fidelity to the real, that is a commitment to remain honest about reality despite suffering or persecution that might come; and (3) a willingness to entertain the possibility of something more, a divine force at work in history. Paulo Freire seemed to embrace the first two dimensions of Sobrino's view of spirituality, but tended to believe the Divine being less involved in the movement of history.

REFERENCES

Bean, W. (2000). Community development and adult education: Locating practice in its roots. *New Directions for Adult and Continuing Education, 83*, 67–76.

Bellah, R., Madsen, R., Sullivan, W., Swidler, A., & Tipton, S. (1985). *Habits of the heart: Individualism and commitment in American life*. New York, NY: Harper and Row.

Berry, T. (1990). *The dream of the earth*. San Francisco, CA: Sierra Club Books.

Boyd, D. (2012). The critical spirituality of Paulo; Freire. *International Journal of Lifelong Education, 31*(6), 759–778.

Dantley, M. (2003). Critical spirituality: Enhancing transformative leadership through critical theory and African American prophetic spirituality. *International Journal of Leadership in Education, 6*(1), 3–17.

Dantley, M. (2005). African American spirituality and Cornel West's notions of prophetic pragmatism. *Education Administration Quarterly, 41*(4), 651–674.

De Kadt, E. (1970). *Catholic radicals in Brazil*. London: Oxford University Press.

Elias, J. (1976a). *Conscientization and deschooling: Freire and Illich's proposals for reshaping society.* Philadelphia, PA: Westminster Press.

Elias, J. (1976b). Paulo Freire: Religious educator. *Religious Education, LXXI*(1), 40–56.

Elias, J. (1994). *Paulo Freire: Pedagogue of liberation*. Malabar, FL: Krieger Publishing.

English, L., & Gillen, M. (2000). Editor's notes. *New Directions for Adult & Continuing Education, 85*(Spring), 1–5.

Fowler, J. (1981). *Stages of faith: The psychology of human development and the quest for meaning.* New York, NY: HarperCollins.

Freire, P. (1970). *Pedagogy of the oppressed* (M. B. Ramos, Trans.). New York, NY: Seabury Press.

Freire, P. (1972). Letter to a young theology student. *LADOC* 3, (29a), 11–12.

Freire, P. (1984). Education, liberation and the church. *Religious Education, 79*(4), 524–545.

Freire, P. (1996). *Letters to Cristina: Reflections on my life and work*. London: Routledge.

Freire, P. (1997). *Pedagogy of the heart* (D. Macedo & A. Oliveira, Trans.). New York, NY: Continuum.

Gotz, I. (1997). On spirituality and teaching. *Philosophy of education*. Retrieved April 15, 2004, from www.ed.uiuc.edu/EPS/PES-Yearbook/97_docs/gotz.html

Gutiérrez, G. (1971). *A theology of liberation: History, politics and salvation* (Sr. C. Inda & J. Eagleson, Trans.). Maryknoll, NY: Orbis Books.

Gutiérrez, G. (2003). *We drink from our own wells: The spiritual journey of a people, 20th anniversary edition* (M. J. O'Connell, Trans.). Maryknoll, NY: Orbis Books.

Hill, P., Pargament, K., Hood Jr, R., McCullough, M., Swyers, J., Larson, D., & Zinnbauer, B. (2000). Conceptualizing religions and spirituality: Points of commonality, points of departure. *Journal for the Theory of Social Behavior, 30*(1), 51–77.

Horton, M., & Freire, P. (1990). *We make the road by walking: Conversations on education and social change* (1st ed., B. Bell, J. Gaventa, & J. Peters, Ed.). Philadelphia, PA: Temple University Press.

Jeria, J. (1986). Vagabond of the obvious: A bibliography of Paulo Freire. *Vitae Scholastica, 5*(1), 1–126.

Keating, A. (2008). I am a citizen of the universe: Gloria Anzaldua's spiritual activism as a catalyst for social change. *Feminist Studies, 34*(1–2), 53–70.

Kirkendall, A. (2004). Entering history: Paulo Freire and the politics of the Brazilian Northeast, 1958–1964. *Luso-Brazilian Review, 41*(1), 168–189.

Kirylo, J. (2012). *Paulo Freire: The man from Recife*. New York, NY: Peter Lang.

Neuhouser, K. (1989). The radicalization of the Brazilian Catholic Church in comparative perspective. *American Sociological Review, 54*(2), 233–244.

Neumann, J. (2011). Critical pedagogy and faith. *Educational Theory, 61*(5), 601–619.

Niebuhr, R. (1927). *Does civilization need religion?* New York, NY: The Macmillan Company.

Purpel, D. (1989). *The moral and spiritual crisis in education: A curriculum for justice and compassion in education*. New York, NY: Bergin & Garvey.

Sobrino, J. (1988). *Spirituality of liberation: Toward political holiness*. (R. B. Barr, Trans.). Maryknoll, NY: Orbis Books.

Stoney, G. (1996). *Paulo Freire & George Stoney church conversation*. Retrieved https://www.youtube.com/watch?v=U8aExMg8foA

Tisdell, E. (2000). Spirituality and emancipatory adult education in women adult educators for social change. *Adult Education Quarterly, 50*(4), 308–335.

Tisdell, E., & Tolliver, D. (2006). Spirituality in the transformative higher education classroom. *New Directions for Adult and Continuing Education, 109*, 37–47.

West, C., & Buschendorf, C. (2016). *Black prophetic fire*. Boston, MA: Beacon Press.

Zwissler, L. (2007). Spiritual but religious: Spirituality among religiously motivated feminist activists. *Culture and Religion, 8*(1), 51–69.

CHAPTER 2

THE EASTER EXPERIENCE

Conversion to the People

DISCOVERING POWERLESSNESS

In his book, *The Soloist, Los Angeles Times* reporter Steve Lopez (2008) tells the moving story of his relationship with a homeless man named Nathanael Ayers. Ayers is a Cleveland-born Juilliard School of Music graduate who develops schizophrenia and ends up homeless in Los Angeles playing his violin on the streets. One day Lopez encounters Ayers and is moved by the beautiful music coming from the violin of this bedraggled homeless man. He goes back to talk to him in the square in which he first heard him and cannot find him. Three weeks later he sees him in the same spot, "his strings barely audible in the orchestra of horns, trucks and sirens" (p. 3). Lopez engages him and there begins an "unlikely friendship" between the two.

For Lopez the relationship begins as an opportunity to write a series of personal interest columns about this classically trained musician playing his violin openly and for free, the kind of music played in high-end music halls frequented by the well-heeled elite of Los Angeles. While in one way the book tells the story of a caring reporter who befriends and seeks to help a needy homeless man, from another perspective the book is about the transformation Lopez needed to go through in order to understand and appreciate the unique gifts of Nathanael Ayers. The series of articles Lopez writes brings attention to Ayer's plight, so much so that one reader is moved to donate a used cello to Ayers. Through Lopez's intervention, Ayers gets to hear the LA Symphony practicing and then to meet with and play alongside a cellist in the Symphony. Lopez is also able to secure an apartment in a facility specifically designed to support those struggling with mental illness and Ayers is able to get off the street. Yet Ayers at times seems unaware and ungrateful for the assistance he has been given, goes AWOL, acts unpredictably, and even lashes out violently at Lopez. Despite his good and honorable intentions, Lopez becomes exasperated with his inability to provide the stable life Lopez longs for Ayers to have.

In the movie version of the book by the same title (Fisher & Wright, 2009), after Ayers has a violent outburst, Lopez (played by Robert Downey, Jr.) sits dejected on his living room couch talking to his wife about all his failures, and says "I thought I was going to help someone… inevitably it backfired. And the person I was trying to be of some redeeming service to turns on me. I'm the enemy, a stranger, and I don't know who to fault. I can't see any outcome to support a belief in anything worthwhile. I'm done trying. I resign, I resign from everything." Lopez has given up and feels like a total failure.

His wife lies on the couch listening to her husband's lament, and then delivers the most poignant line in the story. She says: "You're never going to cure Nathanael. Just be a friend and show up." While Lopez was trying to help, what Ayers actually needed and ultimately wanted was Lopez simply to be with him in whatever circumstances he found himself. At this point of great frustration and powerlessness, where he faces his inability to fix a broken, confused homeless man that has become part of his life, Steve Lopez has what Paulo Freire calls an Easter Experience.

CONVERSION TO THE PEOPLE

In *Pedagogy of the Oppressed* Freire (1993) discusses the attitude and perspective of revolutionary leaders toward the people they feel moved to help achieve liberation from their oppressors. He notes that while these leaders truly desire to bring about revolutionary change, they usually come from the oppressor class, and as a result "they almost always bring with them the marks of their origin: their prejudices and their deformations, which include a lack of confidence in the ability of the people's ability to think, to want and to know" (p. 60). For Freire, "trusting the people is the indispensable precondition for revolutionary change" (p. 60). This lack of authentic trust in the people's ability to participate fully in their liberation can inadvertently cause leaders to use the methods of the oppressor to achieve their liberatory ends. These methods include such approaches as conquest, coercion, manipulation, and cultural invasion; by their very nature these methods treat people as objects to be moved rather than self-authorizing subjects of their own lives and destinies. Freire goes to great lengths in chapter four of *Pedagogy of the Oppressed* to illuminate the distinction between revolutionary leaders working *for* or acting *on* the people as opposed to working and acting *with* the people. Even in leaders' good intentions of working toward the liberation of the people, if the people themselves do not have a critical role in the liberation process, in the end they remain objects and revolutionary leaders have simply exchanged one form of oppression for another. For Freire, the means by which revolution is achieved -dialogue and praxis – must be consistent with the revolutionary ends they seek.

In order for revolutionary leaders, who to varying degrees have "the oppressor housed within them" (p. 135) to be effective in their efforts at liberation, there must be a profound internal change, which Freire calls a "conversion to the people" (p. 61), and which enables these leaders to enter into "communion with the people". He goes on to describe the process this way:

> Conversion to the people requires a profound rebirth. Those who undergo it
> take on a new form of existence; they can no longer remain as they were.
> through comradeship with the oppressed can the converts understand

their characteristic ways of living and behaving, which in diverse moments reflect the structure of domination. One of those characteristics is the previously mentioned existential duality of the oppressed, who are at the same time themselves and the oppressor whose image they have internalized. (p. 61)

Later, reiterating the same idea, Freire simply says "in the revolutionary process there is only one way for the emerging leaders to achieve authenticity: they must 'die' in order to be reborn through and with the oppressed" (p. 133).

In essence what Freire is saying is that in order for well-meaning leaders to work for substantive and radical social change, they must go through a profound internal change in terms of their values and perspectives, particularly as they relate to the people these leaders feel compelled to help. They have to come to terms with their "inner oppressor" and make every effort to see, act, and think in ways distinctly different from how they were raised and socialized to think, see, and act. He makes clear that simple awareness of one's inner oppressor is not enough. He writes:

[An individual] discovering himself to be an oppressor may cause considerable anguish, but it does not necessarily lead to solidarity with the oppressed, ... Solidarity requires that one enter into the situation of those with whom one is solidary; it is a radical posture... true solidarity with the oppressed means fighting at their side to transform the objective reality which has made them these 'beings for another.' (Freire, 1993, p. 49)

While Freire does not speak of this transformation in spiritual terms, he does use the distinctly religious term "conversion" to describe the process, even invoking the Biblical concept of resurrection by speaking of dying and being reborn.[1]

In *Politics of Education*, Freire (1985) expands on this insight and refers to this transformational process as a person's "Easter." In a chapter entitled "Education, Liberation and the Church" he discusses the role of the church in the liberation of the people from their oppression; given his Latin American context, we can assume that he is thinking primarily of the priests and lay leaders in the Roman Catholic Church. He rejects the oft-noted idea that the Church can and should remain politically neutral; to do so is to implicitly support the status quo. He also rejects the belief that in doing acts of service the church can help the oppressed to become free of their oppression. Such a perspective is "an anesthetic or aspirin practices ... that can only lead to the preservation of the status quo" (p. 122).

Even those in their well-meaning naiveté, who renounce the ideals and values of the oppressor class, can continue unwittingly to practice the ways of the oppressive, dominator class. In order to truly join with the oppressed, they must enter an "apprenticeship" in which they are severely tested. Freire (1985) describes the apprenticeship this way:

The *sine qua non* the apprenticeship demands is that, first of all, they really experience their own Easter, that they die as elitists so as to be resurrected on the side of the oppressed, that they be born again with the beings who were

15

d to be… This Easter, which results in a changing of consciousness,
xistentially experienced. The real Easter is not commemorative
is praxis, it is historical involvement. (pp. 122–123)

In other words, there is both a change in thought patterns and behavior, which is ongoing and mutually reinforcing. The thought dimension of this change involves the "renunciation of myths" that the individual has imbibed, such as one's belief in inherent superiority, the neutrality of the church and its teachings, the inferiority of the poor, and the belief that they are fixed to their oppressed condition by fate, God, ignorance or their flawed character. The behavioral dimension, or praxis, involves actively participating with the oppressed in their efforts at liberation while continuing to reflect and learn more about themselves and the conditions that have created the oppression. For Freire this notion of an Easter is not just a mental change of perspective or symbolic recognition of a need to change, but rather is grounded in concrete, visible actions and commitments. The change in thought and perspective leads one to a change in behavior, which in turn introduces one to new experiences and insights, thus deepening and informing one's thoughts and perspective.

When speaking of educators, Freire maintains a similar view. In *Letters to Cristina* (1996), he insists that the one who teaches must seek to "shorten the distance between what he or she says and does" (p. 162). In other words, teachers must not simply teach about democratic values and freedom, they must embody those ideals in their actions and their very person. Like the revolutionaries and religious folks described in the earlier texts, here he makes the same charge for those who aspire to be revolutionary educators, preparing students to change the world, rather than just fit in. He writes:

No doubt racist, sexist, and elitist teachers who speak about democracy and call themselves progressive must become truly committed to freedom, must undergo their own Easter. They must die to their old selves as sexists, racists, and elitists and be reborn as true progressives, enlisted in the struggle for the reinvention of the world. What is not possible is to continue in the ambiguity that their incoherence brings on – progressive discourse, reactionary practice. (p. 163)

This bringing together of one's revolutionary values and liberatory actions happens through the process of an individual's Easter experience, a deep inner transformation that leads to a similar transformation in one's liberatory practice.

FREIRE'S EASTER

Though Freire never refers specifically to his own Easter, given his commitment to praxis, one can reasonably assume that this concept arose in part out of his own experience. Furthermore, while he does not refer much to his own spiritual beliefs or practices, his use of overtly religious terms like "conversion," "Easter"

and "death and rebirth," suggests that there may have been some
inner transformation had a spiritual dimension to it (see Chapter
few explicitly theological writings, "A Letter to a Young Theology Stuᴜᴜ...
Freire talks about Christians hearing the Word of God, which is "inviting me ᴜ
recreate the world" and which causes people "to make themselves subjects, agents
of their salvation and liberation" (p. 12). However he goes on to say because the
way in which the non-oppressed have been socialized to think in oppressive ways,
they are unable to hear the liberating Word of God. In order to hear that Word the
non-oppressed must "undergo an Easter." Throughout the letter Freire refers to "we
Christians" indicating that he saw himself undergoing the same process he describes
that others must undergo.

Indeed, Freire's Easter and conversion to the people began at an early age. In
Letters to Cristina, (1996) he talks a great deal about his childhood experience and
his family's descent from a middle class lifestyle to a life of poverty after his father's
illness and eventual death during the global Great Depression in the late 1920s and
early 1930s. He said that although his family had descended to the "deepest level
of need," they had a "hidden poverty" because of their middle class values and
outlooks, as well as the presence of a piano in their home and his father's insistence
on wearing neckties (p. 42). These signs and trappings of middle class life made
them appear to be better off than they actually were. At the same time, as a boy he
listened to his father and uncle discuss the social and political issues of the day,
and at an early age absorbed the notion that the oppressed's belief in God would
eventually empower them to achieve their liberation. With that informal education at
his father's knee and his own experience of poverty, he clearly saw himself as better
off than many of his peers and felt compelled to pursue a life of service to those who
were poor and downtrodden.

In *Pedagogy of Hope*, Freire (1992) tells a story that in some ways could be
evidence of his own ongoing Easter. Early in his career as an educator, he was giving
a public talk on how to discipline children in school and in the home; he based
his remarks on the research of the Swiss psychologist Jean Piaget. The gist of his
talk was that parents should seek to develop a "dialogical, loving relationship" with
their children, rather than trying simply to control their behavior through the use of
corporal punishment.

Following the talk, a man stood to ask a question. Freire described him as a
man in his forties "already worn out and exhausted" by the strains of life. After
sarcastically praising Freire for his lofty presentation, he put a piercing question to
him: "Dr. Paulo, sir—do you know where people live? Have you ever been to their
houses?" The man went on to describe the cramped and impoverished conditions in
which he and others of that community lived. He highlighted the contrast between
his living conditions and the relatively comfortable, spacious and well-resourced
nature of Freire's home. He then concluded "If people hit their kids and even 'go
beyond bounds' as you say, it's not because people don't love their kids. No, it is
because life is so hard, they don't have much choice" (pp. 24–26).

17

Freire referred to that experience as "the clearest and most bruising lesson I have ever received in my life as an educator" (p. 24). He realized he had been "[oblivious to] the hard reality of the huge audience seated before [him]" (p. 23). Without minimizing the horrors of domestic violence and child abuse, he realized that as an educator he needed to understand the world of the people he was trying to reach and help. He could not just speak *to* people; rather he need to join *with* them in the concrete circumstances of their difficult lives. Out of such experiences, Freire developed a pedagogical philosophy focused on learning about the lived reality of the people he was teaching to read, spending time with them in the fields, developing vocabulary words and phonemes out of their daily activities, and only then teaching them how to read. He called this approach "reading the word and reading the world" (Freire & Macedo, 1987). It all started with what he would later refer to as an Easter experience.

EASTER EXPERIENCE AS AN ONGOING PROCESS

While Freire did not write in depth on the nature of the internal process he called "conversion to the people" and the Easter experience, others have. In fact, the concept of conversion to the people is relative to the notion of conversion to the poor, which is foundational to the liberation theology movement that emerged out of Latin America in the 1970s. Speaking of the dramatic changes in theological thinking arising after Vatican II, Peruvian liberation theologian Gustavo Gutiérrez (1984), who also was a good friend of Freire, writes that for Latin American Christians, following Jesus is integrally related to sharing the experience of the poor in their midst. He goes on to say that this new emphasis on the gospel to and with the poor caused many in the Roman Catholic Church to rethink and reconsider their long held spiritual traditions.[2] Gutiérrez points out that it was this conversion to the poor that enabled El Salvadoran Archbishop Oscar Romero to share a powerful testimony only two weeks before his assassination by government soldiers: "My life has been threatened many times. I have to confess that as a Christian, I don't believe in death without resurrection. If they kill me, I will rise again in the Salvadoran people" (p. 32).

Like Freire, Gutiérrez calls the process by which one enters into solidarity with the poor "conversion." Conversion in Gutiérrez's view is an ongoing, lifelong process, in which one is continually invited to live a life of faithfulness to God. This conversion is not just an internal, private response, but impacts the whole of one's life. Commenting on Gutiérrez's view of conversion, Sobrino (1988) writes that this conversion causes one "to enter into another universe, the world of the poor" (p. 63). One must acknowledge his or her sin, which in the main is choosing to pay attention and be aware of the struggles and sufferings of others, as well as refraining from thoughts, attitudes, and behavior that dehumanizes others.[3]

Freire saw the Easter experience as central to what it means to be a Christian. He wrote: "[The Easter experience] demands that we die and be born again. Every Christian must live his Easter… The man [sic] who doesn't make his Easter, in the sense of dying to be reborn, is no real Christian" (Freire, 1974, p. 30). In this way we see that for Freire faith and politics, spirituality and social practice, were not separate realms, but integrally related to one another. One's spiritual commitment was intimately related to one's willingness to join the oppressed in their struggle for liberation, and to do that they had to die to self materially, culturally, politically and spiritually.

STAGES OF CONVERSION TO THE POOR

Roman Catholic priest Albert Nolan (1985) sought to describe this process of conversion out of his work with the oppressed in South African townships under apartheid. Nolan (1985) outlines a four-stage process "of what takes place in our common journey towards maturity in the service of the poor" (p. 3). Nolan writes out of his own experience and reflects on the changes that took place in his perspective while he worked among the poor in the townships. In so doing, he provides a guide for those embarking or being drawn to solidarity with the poor through the Easter experience.

Nolan says that the first stage of one's journey in service to the poor is characterized by *compassion.* One becomes aware of the needs of others and, while wanting to act, must confront all the reasonable excuses why one would and should not change one's life in order to serve the poor. Eventually compassion wins out, and one chooses to act concretely, usually doing some sort of charitable or relief work like distributing food or giving money to a cause.

As one enters the second stage of the process, there is a growing awareness that the needs one is seeking to address are rooted in unjust laws, policies, and practices. This realization of the structural nature of poverty leads one to *anger* at the rich, at politicians, at government and at authority figures in one's life who neither told of these things nor did anything to correct them. One realizes that the people are relatively powerless to change the systems and are simply at the mercy of these systems regardless of whether they accept or reject them. The system must be changed, and so the focus moves from simply providing relief to working to bring about substantive change in the structures that oppress.

As one continues in the struggle for justice, they may enter the third stage in which they realize that the poor and oppressed must liberate themselves, and that the role of the non-oppressed helper is mainly to work alongside them. In this time, anger is accompanied by a deep *humility and admiration* for the poor. One begins to wonder if they need the poor more than the poor need them. While in many ways admirable, this approbation can lead to an unhealthy romanticizing of the poor, taking anything they do or say to be the truth, and believing it is not possible for the poor to do anything wrong or perverse or destructive. However, Nolan warns: "This is the kind of romanticism that does the poor and ourselves no good at all" (p. 8), because one is not seeing people for who they really are.

The fourth and final stage in this conversion process is what Nolan regards as "real solidarity," and which initially is characterized by feelings of *disillusionment and disappointment.* Before one can be in true solidarity with others, one must see and accept them for the complex, imperfect beings they truly are, rather than what one imagines or wishes they would be. However, as solidarity truly takes hold, the perspective moves from "them" and "us" to "we." Nolan also notes that the solidarity of the non-poor with the poor can also lead to a greater solidarity of the poor among themselves. Oppression remains, struggles persist, and suffering continues, yet out of the solidarity arises a strength to challenge those forces with renewed vigor. Nolan concludes: "In the end we will find one another in God – whatever our particular approach to God might be … It is precisely by recognizing the cause of the poor as God's cause that we can come through the crisis of disillusionment and disappointment with particular poor people" (p. 9).

Gutiérrez (2013) stresses that this conversion to solidarity with the poor should not be taken on as individual quest, but rather as something pursued in community with others, presumably others in the church. Central to this position of solidarity is a deep concern for the material needs and oppressive structures assaulting the poor. Further, he notes that this solidarity is not done in some abstract sense, but calls one to be personally involved with "human beings of flesh and bone" (LOC 1473). Moreover, this commitment cannot be occasional or temporary, but must be constant, persistent, and ongoing. Finally, this solidarity is to be bathed in an attitude of gratitude and love for each other and for God. Through this solidarity between poor and non-poor, between people struggling together in community, those involved will encounter Christ in a profound way.

LIBERATING THE OPPRESSOR

The ultimate end of the Easter experience is the liberation of the oppressors from their own dehumanization. Freire (1993) writes:

> As the oppressors dehumanize others and violate their rights, they themselves become dehumanized. As the oppressed, fighting to be human, take away the oppressors' power to dominate and suppress, they restore to the oppressors the humanity they had lost in the exercise of oppression. It is only the oppressed who, by freeing themselves, can free their oppressors. (p. 56)

This same theme is discussed by a number of liberation theologians. James Cone writes: "When the oppressed affirm their freedom by refusing to behave according to the master's rules, they not only liberate themselves from oppression, but they also liberate the oppressors from an enslavement to their illusions" (as quoted in Bucher, 1976, p. 523).

Gustavo Gutiérrez (1971, p. 275) picks up this same refrain when talking about the power of love: "Universal love is that which in solidarity with the oppressed seeks also to liberate the oppressors from their own power, from their ambition and from their selfishness." Finally, Rosemary Reuther echoes the previous writers when she writes, "[Theology] will be looking to what transformations need to take place to transform Christianity from a Constantinian to a prophetic religion, from an ideology of oppression to a gospel of liberation for the oppressed, and through the oppressed for the oppressor as well" (Bucher, 1976, p. 524).

To the outsider such language might seem naïve at best and dangerous at worst— to assume persons or groups accustomed to their power, wealth, and prestige could and would be "converted" to a life of solidarity with the oppressed whom they have directly or indirectly exploited. Other critics might regard these expressions as simply veiled language for some sort of socialist economic reversal. However, Gutiérrez (2013) sees this process as spiritual and concrete at the same time. This move toward solidarity with the oppressed is rooted first and foremost in a deep awareness of the graciousness and generosity of God, and in fact, as an encounter with Christ. While deeply personal and inward, that encounter at the same time is made concrete in a direct relationship with the poor themselves; the spiritual becomes personal, the divine becomes concrete. Poverty becomes real in the form of real persons, and in solidarity with those persons one experiences a deeper encounter with God.[4] Just as the young Freire's encounter with the stressed out farmer-father set him on a different manner of interaction with the poor campesinos he taught to read, so too the Easter experiences of other non-oppressed persons lead them into lives of activism on behalf of the marginalized and oppressed of their era.

EASTER EXPERIENCE TODAY

Freire's writings arose out of a particular historical moment when Latin America began to emerge from an era of colonialism, elitism, and economic exploitation. He was also present during the period when a number of formerly colonized nations, particularly in Africa, were breaking free of their colonial past, and were seeking to reconstruct their denuded societies. When he was thinking and writing about conversion to the poor and the Easter experience, this was his context. So what do these deeply spiritual ideas and processes mean for our day for people of faith and conscience? In what way must we seek the kind of transformative process called for in his own era? Two contemporary examples may be instructive.

PAUL FARMER

Dr. Paul Farmer is the founder of Partners in Health (PIH), which began in a medical clinic in rural Haiti. Farmer grew up in unique circumstances, spending his high school years living on the edge of a swamp with his parents and five siblings. Farmer earned a scholarship to Duke University through the help of his teachers who saw his tremendous academic potential. While at Duke, he was deeply influenced by the assassination of El Salvadoran bishop Oscar Romero, who was killed for his outspoken advocacy on behalf of the poor in that country. He also met Sister Julianna DeWolf in the context of writing a paper about the plight of farmworkers. Through his interaction with her, he became aware of the relative proximity of the desperately poor farmworkers to the luxurious Duke campus. These two experiences moved him to work for social change (Block & Griffin, 2013).

While attending Harvard Medical School, he made a trip to work in a clinic in Haiti, which became the initial site of Partners in Health. He developed a practice living among the poor in Haiti, learning to understand their health challenges, not just from his elite medical training, but also from the perspective of the poor. He would often spend a whole day hiking through the Haitian countryside visiting families to learn their stories, taking in their surroundings, and seeking to understand their lives. Today PIH is an international organization serving thousands of people in over a dozen countries. Dr. Farmer is considered an international expert on HIV/AIDS and Tuberculosis and is called upon to consult around the world (Block & Griffin, 2013).

A practicing Roman Catholic, Dr. Farmer (2013) lives according to what he calls "a theology of accompaniment," a term he developed in conjunction with Gustavo Gutiérrez. Dr. Farmer, while working in and overseeing the development of rural health clinics, is also an outspoken advocate for economic justice, and regularly speaks and writes on health care as a basic human right.

Writing about his early experiences in Haiti, Farmer describes working in a rural clinic with a young Haitian doctor. Farmer was struck by the reality that children and adults were dying from all sorts of diseases he had been trained to cure with certain medicines. Local people attributed these deaths to fate and sorcery. His Haitian counterpart was resigned to his inability to change his patients' situations or their belief systems. Farmer writes: "Not yet thirty, that doctor had been socialized for scarcity and failure.... even as I had been socialized for plenty and success" (LOC 427). Over time and in part due to his reading of Gutiérrez's *Theology of Liberation*, Farmer came to understand that "[p]overty is not some accident of nature, but the result of historically given and economically driven forces" that shape people's worldview. At the same time, he adds: "Understanding poverty.... requires listening to those most affected by poverty" (LOC 475). Listening is not only part of understanding a person's need, but also an approach to research that looks for holistic responses to health needs in places of desperate poverty. Farmer goes on: "the self-styled liberators from poverty are too often those who want to preach, rather than listen, to the poor" (LOC 534).

Paul Farmer, despite his Duke and Harvard education, and despite his world-renowned status, does not start with bringing out his expertise or credentials, but focuses on accompaniment in the form of listening to the poor. In Freire's (1993) terms Farmer has "enter[ed] into the situation of those with whom [he] is solidary; it is a radical posture" (p. 49). He is embodying the Easter Experience.

NEW SANCTUARY MOVEMENT

The New Sanctuary Movement (NSM) is a loose nationwide network of religious communities and concerned individuals that works alongside undocumented immigrants facing deportation. NSM sees its roots in the original Sanctuary

Movement of the 1980s, which hosted refugees and undocumented migrants in local houses of worship. This then gave advocates time to develop legal cases, justifying the migrants' right to stay permanently in the U.S. At the time law enforcement chose not to invade those sacred spaces, and so migrants were safe. The Sanctuary movement itself drew inspiration from the churches that hid Jews being chased by the Nazis and the abolitionist movement of the 1800s in the U.S. At its height the Sanctuary Movement sheltered up to half a million refugees fleeing death squads that were fighting a U.S. proxy war in several Central and South American countries (Lo, 2015).

Today's New Sanctuary Movement seeks to provide a similar type of support to undocumented persons, though law enforcement is far less accommodating. In Philadelphia (PA), NSM has committed itself to engage in immigrant justice campaigns on a local and national level by building connections between local faith communities with members of the undocumented immigrant community. Through concerted campaigns, NSM has convinced political leaders of Philadelphia to declare itself as a Sanctuary City, despite intense pressure from the Federal Government.[5] This means that Philadelphia law enforcement refuses to assist federal agents in their apprehension and prosecution of undocumented individuals (NSMP, 2016).

Philadelphia NSM's main program is called "Accompaniment," in which local congregations are paired with immigrant families facing deportation. The development of relationships between congregation members and families creates a bond of trust and mutuality. Congregations seek to provide legal referrals and organizing groups to accompany individuals to deportation hearings (NSMP, 2016). In 2017 NSM trained over a thousand people for a program called "Sanctuary in the Streets," a rapid response plan to come to the aid of families when a raid by ICE (Immigration and Customs Enforcement) occurs, even in some cases seeking to obstruct ICE from carrying out their mission.

In a recent interview, Peter Pedemonti, director of NSM Philadelphia, stressed the importance of shared leadership, assuring that all groups working in NSM are at least 50% immigrant, and that campaigns and actions are guiding the needs and perceptions of the undocumented folks in the group. For Peter, this approach is deeply rooted in his spirituality, which has been influenced by both Catholicism and Buddhism. He sees himself as part of a larger community of people of faith, undocumented citizens, and a "cloud of witnesses" who have gone before him, which fills him with a sense of hope and a commitment to continue in the struggle for immigrant justice (Duffy, 2016).

Both Paul Farmer, NSM and Peter Pedemonti are contemporary expressions of Freire's concept of the Easter experience. Both Partners in Health and NSM have institutionalized the values of accompaniment and a conversion to be with the poor into their operating principles. Both are clear examples that what Freire calls the non-poor in relationship to the poor is not simply a pedagogical or philosophical or even theological position, but is a worldview and a way of life rooted in a deep sense of spiritual commitment and transcendence.

NOTES

[1] For more on the concept of conversion from a liberation theology perspective see Gustavo Gutiérrez, *We Drink from Our Own Wells* (Orbis. 1995) and *Jon Sobrino Spirituality of Liberation* (Orbis, 1988).

[2] For more on the development of Liberation Theology, see Chapter 8.

[3] Sobrino (1988) builds on these thoughts, stressing that in order for one to be a true liberator of others, one must liberate him/herself first. We must face "the necessity of our own liberation if we are to secure the liberation of our neighbor" (p. 62). This conversion implies that we have sinned both against God and against the poor, and that in converting we are turning toward God and the people in both thought and behavior.

[4] Sobrino (1988, pp. 13–20) conveys a similar sentiment in insisting that the foundation of any authentic approach to spirituality is in his words, engaging an "honesty about the real" and a "fidelity to the real." By the real, he means the concrete, daily struggles of the poor. One's spirituality must be shaped by a deep involvement with those struggles, and must be committed to seek liberation from those struggles over the long haul, regardless of the cost and even loss of life, such solidarity and faithful might entail. At the same time one has engaged in the struggle, one's spirituality is open to the "more of reality," the presence and action of God, aiding in the liberation process.

[5] In November 2016 shortly after the election of Donald Trump to the presidency, James Kenney, the mayor of Philadelphia, began referring to Philadelphia as a Fourth Amendment city saying: "We respect and live up to the Fourth Amendment, which means you can't be held against your will without a warrant from the court signed by a judge" (Terruso, 2016). As a candidate, Mr. Trump had repeatedly called for the wholesale deportation of all estimated 11 million undocumented immigrants residing in the United States.

REFERENCES

Block, J. W., & Griffin, M. (2013). Introduction. In M. Griffin & J. W. Block (Eds.), *In the company of the poor: Conversations between Dr. Paul Farmer and Father Gustavo Gutiérrez* (Kindle Version). Maryknoll, NY: Orbis Books.

Bucher, G. (1976). Toward a liberation theology for the "oppressor." *Journal of the American Academy of Religion, 44*(3), 517–534.

Duffy, K. (2016, April). Interview with Peter Pedemonti, co-founder of New Sanctuary Movement of Philadelphia.

Farmer, P. (2013). Reimangining accompaniment: A doctor's tribute to Gustavo Gutierrez. In J. W. Block & M. Griffin (Eds.), *In the company of the poor: Conversations between Dr. Paul Farmer and Father Gustavo Gutierrez* (Kindle Version, LOC 405–676). Maryknoll, NY: Orbis Books.

Fisher, G. (Producer), & Wright, J. (Director). (2009). *The soloist* (Motion Picture). United States: Paramount Pictures.

Freire, P. (1972). Letter to a young theology student. *LADOC* 3, (29a), 11–12.

Freire, P. (1974). Conscientisation. *Cross Currents*, 23–31.

Freire, P. (1984). Know, practice, teach the gospels [Originally written in 1977]. *Religious Education, 79*(4), 547–548.

Freire, P. (1985). Education, liberation and the church. In P. Freire (Ed.), *The politics of education: Culture, power and liberation* (D. Macedo, Trans., 1st ed., pp. 121–144). Westport, CT: Bergin & Garvey.

Freire, P. (1992). *Pedagogy of hope: Reliving the pedagogy of the oppressed.* New York, NY: Continuum.

Freire, P. (1993). *Pedagogy of the oppressed: 30th anniversary edition* (M. B. Ramos, Trans.). New York, NY: Continuum.

Freire, P. (1996). *Letters to Cristina: Reflections on my life and work.* London: Routledge.

Freire, P., & Macedo, D. (1987). *Literacy: Reading the word, reading the world.* New York, NY: Bergin & Garvey.

Gutiérrez, G. (1971). *A theology of liberation: History, politics and salvation* (Sr. C. Inda & J. Eagleson, Trans.). Maryknoll, NY: Orbis.

Gutiérrez, G. (1984). *We drink from our own wells: The spiritual journey of a people*. Maryknoll, NY: Orbis Books.

Gutiérrez, G. (2013). Conversion: A requirement for solidarity. In M. Griffin & J. W. Block (Eds.), *In the company of the poor: Conversations between Dr. Paul Farmer and Father Gustavo Gutiérrez* (Kindle Version). Maryknoll, NY: Orbis Books, Loc 1326-1742.

Lo, P. (2015). Inside the new sanctuary movement that's protecting immigrants from ICE: Can a network of churches fight deportations. *The Nation, 300*(21), 20–24.

Lopez, S. (2008). *The soloist*. New York, NY: Berkely Trade/Penguin.

New Sanctuary Movement of Philadelphia. (2016). *Who we are*. Retrieved from http://sanctuaryphiladelphia.org/

Nolan, A. (1985). *The service of the poor and spiritual growth*. London, UK: Catholic Institute for International Relations.

Partners in Health. (2016). *Countries*. Retrieved from http://www.pih.org/countries

Sobrino, J. (1988). *Spirituality of liberation: Toward political holiness*. Maryknoll, NY: Orbis Books.

Terruso, J. (2016, November 10). Kenney: Philadelphia to remain a sanctuary city – for now. *Philly. com*. Retrieved at http://www.philly.com/philly/blogs/heardinthehall/Kenney-Philadelphia-will-stay-sanctuary-city---for-now.html

PERSONALISM, HUMANISM, AND
A FREIREAN SPIRITUALITY TOWARD
HUMANIZING HUMANITY

Concern for humanization leads at once to the recognition of dehumanization, not only as an ontological possibility but as an historical reality. And as man perceives the extent of dehumanization, he asks himself if humanization is a viable possibility.

(Freire, 1990, p. 27)

From the French Catholic personalist philosopher Emmanuel Mounier he [Freire] gleans his extremely important theme of 'the humanization of man,' which refers to an inherently progressive and optimistic view of human history.

(Elias, 1994, p. 33)

At the turn of the 12th century Giovanni di Bernardone of Assisi, a young aspiring knight, was taken prisoner between the warring Assisi and Perugia in the Umbria region in central Italy. Enduring approximately a year in the harsh conditions of prison, Giovanni di Bernardone (better known as Francesco) was released through a ransom payment, as his father was a wealthy textile merchant. Coming home extremely sick, it was during his road to recovery that Francesco experienced a deep conversion, leading him to abandon his dream to participate in the crusades, to leave behind his youthful excesses of partying, and to not follow in his father's footsteps as a textile merchant.

Instead, Francesco was profoundly moved to radically live a life of poverty, chastity, and obedience. This was much to the raging chagrin of his father, Pietro Bernardone, who in an effort to humiliate Francesco, beat him, and shamed him by dragging Francesco to the resident of the local Bishop with bystanders in watch. Pietro's hope was that the bishop would admonish Francesco for his disobedience to his father. Instead, as the story is told, with great tranquility, publically renouncing all worldly possessions, Francesco removes all the fine clothes off his back, hands them over to his bewildered father and to the amazement of the bishop and onlookers, departs Assisi to embrace his new life.

Francis of Assisi is arguably one of the most recognized religious figures who has captured the adulation of those in a cross-section of religious and non-religious circles. He is often portrayed as the saint of the poor, along with being the patron saint of animals and ecology. As discussed in Chapter 8, Cardinal Jorge Mario

27

Bergoglio of Argentina took on the name Francis as his pontifical title in recognition of Francis of Assisi and his commitment to the poor.

While certainly countless other examples can be made, another figure who was deeply influenced by Francis of Assisi was Peter Maurin, founder of the Catholic Worker Movement in the 1930s. With its presence still active today, the Catholic Worker Movement (along with their periodical *The Catholic Worker*) is one that remains committed to non-violence, ministering to the poor, and justice. While Maurin was the founder of the movement, it was Dorothy Day who famously placed an indelible face on it. Day not only made clear that Maurin would remind followers that Francis of Assisi was the model of inspiration, but also that Maurin introduced the movement to the French philosopher Emmanuel Mounier (1905–1950) and his concept of personalism.[1] Even taking it further, Day (1945) declared that Francis of Assisi "…was most truly the 'great personalist'" (para 1).

Whether it is Francis of Assisi penned as the great personalist or Pope Francis who speaks from personalist thought or Dorothy Day and Peter Maurin who were integral in incorporating personalism in the Catholic Worker Movement, it should be no surprise, therefore, with such like-minded luminaries that Paulo Freire, too, is among that number who identifies with personalism. To that end, because personalism has had a critical influential character on those towering individuals—and more particularly in the case of Freire—this chapter will begin with a discussion of the concept of personalism, that which is principally linked to the work of Emmanuel Mounier. Indeed, to understand Freire's conception of personalism is to be aware of Mounier's influence. And because personalism possesses a natural association with humanist thought, this link will naturally be integrated in this discussion, as well. Finally, this chapter will tie the collective latter with the thought of Freire.

PERSONALISM AND ITS EXPLICABLE LINK TO HUMANISM

The etymology of the word "person" comes from the Latin *persona*, naturally signifying person or human being, but also one taking on the role of a character or a mask and to "sound through" that *personare* (also from the Latin) in order to magnify one's voice as in an open Roman theater. The notion of persona was a critical, and often contentious, subject in the early Christian church as it related to the trinity, and the mystery of explaining one God represented in three "persons," as in God the father, God the son, and God the Holy Spirit.

Explaining early on the intersection between the divine and humanity in the trinity, Boethius (c.480–524), who was the first to notably provide a definition of personhood, contends that the notion of person is "an individual substance of a rational nature," which provides an inclusive description in which the divine is intimately linked to the individual. That is, the innermost part of the person, the rational is that part in which the spiritual emerges. While complex in nature and beyond the scope of purpose for a detailed discussion here, the idea of personhood and its tie to the spiritual is one in which one can discern good from evil and truth from falsity (Williams & Bengtsson, 2016; Koterski, 2012). To be sure, personalists view with great significance the link between humanity and the spiritual, underscoring "…both the dignity that attaches to all persons by virtue of rationality and the status of persons as individual beings or substances" (Koterski, 2012, para 2).

Personalism, albeit, is not a singular system of thinking or a solitary attitude, but rather a philosophy (Mounier, 1952), making it, therefore, a challenging concept to define because there are a variety of "personalisms." For example, there are strands of personalism that are European, North American, Latin American, Eastern, and African, representing an array of personalistic branches that include realistic personalists and idealistic personalists (subdivided into personal idealists, ethical personalists, absolutistic personalists, and panpsychistic personalists) (Buford, n.d.; Williams & Bengtsson, 2016).[2]

However, within all the strands of personalism, the centrality of the person, the uniqueness of personhood, and the relational intersection of persons is fundamental. In other words, the lift off point of ontological and epistemological reflection begins with the person, critically examining the dignity, status, and experience of what it means to be human. And while personalism is not only linked to the metaphysical, and possesses an integral link to the spiritual and belief in God, this does not suggest that all personalists are theists or believers in a god(s) (Williams & Bengtsson, 2016).

For personalists there is a distinct difference between persons and non-persons; that is, there is an exceptionalism of the human person from all other life forms. This exceptionalism not only suggests that human beings are more than matter, more than an animal and distinctly different from animals, but also that each and every human being is unique unto herself/himself. In other words, a person is a "somebody, not a "something;" a "subject," not an "object" (Williams & Bengtsson, 2016).

Therefore, whether it is the poem *I Am – Somebody*, written by civil rights activist Reverend William Holmes Borders, Sr.;[3] the work of Paulo Freire when he underscores the critical importance of person as active subjects of history (to be discussed later); or the writings of Martin Buber (1958), as mentioned in Chapter 5 when he makes the distinction between an *I-thou* relationship to an *I-it* relationship, all are stressing the significance of community and the "somebodiness" of each individual in that community.

Hence, a central aspect of personalism is affirming the dignity of each person, which naturally intersects with the notion of justice, a cardinal virtue that is also discussed in Chapter 5. And while personalism underscores the uniqueness of each person, it also realizes that human beings are social beings, and a harmonized interdependence among persons is vital whereby humanity is perfected (Williams & Bengtsson, 2016).

EMMANUEL MOUNIER

During the first half of the 20th Century, Paris, Munich, and Lublin were critical higher learning centers in Europe where personalists particularly gathered. It was during the time frame in which Europe was confronted with economic disarray, political and moral confusion, a traditionalist institutional church, and in which the masses found little comfort in the materialism and individualist roots of the bourgeois, and reacted to the determinism, rationalism, and the absolute idealism of Georg Hegel. As a response to this European reality (c. between WWI-WWII), it was Emmanuel Mounier (1905–1950) from the Parisian group who emerged as a leader of personalist thought with his founding of the journal *Esprit* (founded 1932 along with Jacques Maritain and Gabriel Marcel) (Williams & Bengtsson, 2016; Sawchenko, 2013; Inglis, 1959).[4]

Contrary to the existentialism of Jean-Paul Sarte (1889–1973) who was more focused on the individualism of personhood, Mounier, naturally drawing from existential and phenomenological thought and deeply influenced by his Catholic faith, promoted a personalism that looked to the interiority of the person, the spiritual being in which human beings are active subjects of history. That is, for Mounier, the person as a spiritual being acting as subject implies that one is not an object, but rather one who exists through action, moving the subjective self from the center in order to realize that purposeful existence occurs through relationship with the other (Williams & Bengtsson, 2016; Sawchenko, 2013; Inglis, 1959).[5]

Unlike individualism, which is fundamentally a philosophy of isolation and self–absorption,[6] the concept of personalism, while realizing the self in personhood, is a constant dynamic to move outside of the self to therefore provide the opening to enter into the challenges that cause human beings to struggle and thus work toward "humanizing" humanity (Mounier, 1952). In this light, therefore, while existentialism can somewhat tend to come from a depressed, anxiety–filled disposition and one that centrally focuses on interior development as the fundamental purpose of existence, personalism, on the other hand, is essentially a humanist philosophy that claims human beings are not determinant, but rather, as alluded above, those where the centrality of the person as subject is the beginning point for ontological and epistemological reflection, acting as a participant in life—rather than spectator—and in participative relationships with others (Williams & Bengtsson, 2016; Sawchenko, 2013; Eneau, 2008; Inglis, 1959).

Mounier's response to early 20th century European economic, social, and institutional religious turmoil was the antithesis of Nietzsche's notion of "God is dead" and that religion was for the weak or Marx's assertion that religion was the "opiate for the masses." While clearly recognizing that class struggle and economic inequities were real, Mounier did not view that utopia would be found in simply finding the solution to economic realities; nor, was the solution to be found in the political establishment and the traditional church. Seeking to reinvent the church and French society, Mounier was looking for a more authentic revitalization or revolution of a new humanism in which the bourgeois would yield to an authentic Christianity, suggesting a lived faith that was renewed in community and in which there was a denunciation of the old (Williams & Bengtsson, 2016; Sawchenko, 2013), and a move toward growing the Kingdom of God in which "…the new man is therefore called upon to make a new earth and the world of the body is asked to put forth its strength, not merely to declare the glory of God, but also to create it" (Mounier, 1995, para 7).

INFORMED BY HUMANIST THOUGHT

To be sure, Mounier's concept of personalism was informed by a humanist philosophy in which he argued that "...humanism is a will to totality," suggesting there is a oneness or a reuniting of "...body and spirit, meditation and operation, thought and action" (pp. 182–183).[7] Although evidence of a humanist philosophy can be traced back earlier, the generally accepted origination of humanism can be dated back to the 14th century, during the era of the European Renaissance, where the concept of individualism, worth, thought, capacity, dignity, and human concern were emphasized as opposed to the religious or theological thinking that drove perspective and interpretation of reality (Komonchak, Collins, & Lane, 1987).[8]

Similar to the case in describing personalism and in addition to broadly splitting it into secular and theological/religious camps, humanism can be challenging to define concretely because over time multiple perspectives have driven its meaning. In the 1800s and from a secular perspective, Ludwig Feuerbach, who was a critical link from the thinking of Georg Hegel to Karl Marx, was highly critical of religion and more specifically of Christianity, promoting a materialistic humanism. Marx furthered Feuerbach's thought with his concept of dialectical materialism, leading to a strand of Marxism known as "Marxist humanism." In short, the foundation of secular humanism remains rooted in the thinking of the Enlightenment (i.e., "I think, therefore I am"-Descartes), depends on the evidence of empirical science, and rejects the supernatural, looking to the collective wisdom of individuals in the move toward a more just social reality and the common good (Kirylo, 2011).

As a response to the secular nature of humanist philosophy, however, it was Karl Barth who argued that authentic humanism is not possible without the infusion of the Gospel message as its foundation. Moreover, Jacques Maritain, a Neo–Thomist and one who was strongly influenced by Henri Bergson, argued for what he characterizes as "integral humanism," making the point that a humanism that leaves the spiritual dimension out of the make–up of what it means to be human would thus amount to a partial humanism (Kirylo, 2011).

Thus, authentic humanism is one that necessarily "integrates" the spiritual as a critical aspect into the description of what it means to be a whole person, indicative of the thinking of Mounier, and still other Christian thinkers such as Teilhard de Chardin and Karl Rahner. And while there is naturally a distinct foundational difference between secular and Christian humanism (and other strands of humanism), all humanist thought is fundamentally grounded in a love for life, is socially conscious, takes responsibility, seeks to explore and discover new knowledge, new adventures, and works to ascertain solutions to human problems and challenges (Kirylo, 2011; Cunningham, 1987; Edwords, n.d.).

MAKING VISIBLE IN PRACTICE THE SPIRITUAL NATURE
OF GOD IN HUMANIZING HUMANITY

In a "Letter to Paulo Freire" Balduino A. Andreola (2004) writes that Freire possessed "…a Christianity of the strong" as that "…envisioned by Mounier in his book *L'Affrontement Chrétien*" (p. xxxix).[9] To put more concretely, Freire's concept of hope (see Chapter 4), his perspective in which God acts in history (see Chapter 8), and his view of utopia (briefly discussed later; also see Chapter 4) are richly grounded in the work of Mounier. That is, critical to Mounier's thought was that the incarnation of God was not only in the person of Jesus, but also manifested in believers who work in community in the image of love, justice, and unity. In this light, therefore, for Freire, history is not predetermined, but rather human beings—as active subjects of history—are in a continuous state of becoming in recreating the world in which the humanization of humanity is cultivated.[10] Indeed, the concept of humanizing humanity is a Mounierean perspective of history that is more progressive and optimistic (Elias, 1994), but yet is one that acknowledges the very real existential threat of dehumanization.

Indeed, from the beginning, as he outlined in his seminal text, *Pedagogy of the Oppressed*, Freire's principal preoccupation with his life's work focused on the dialectical nature between humanization and dehumanization.[11] And to respond to his rhetorical question in the epigraph at the beginning of this chapter if humanization is a viable possibility, Freire argues to move toward that end, humanization (or transformative change) is fostered in a counter–hegemonic process where one does not escape from history, but rather embraces and acts in history. That is, the oppressed (or those subjected to dehumanizing conditions) should

> …never be seen as a group to be led nor as individuals in need of salvation by a vanguard, but rather as creators of their own liberation…this level of respect and love for all means that each individual must be the maker of her or his own liberation. There can be no liberation—that is truly liberating—that is imposed from above, no matter how good the intentions. (Fraser, 1997, pp. 176–177)

Stated another way and particularly revolutionary for those that have historically been living in the shadows, history does not need to be fixed or predetermined; rather history is a possibility; it can be made, invented and reinvented (Freire, 1997). The engagement of the oppressed in their movement toward becoming subject is rooted in Freire's conviction that humanization (or becoming more fully human) is an ontological vocation and, moreover, implies the political nature embedded in the process (Freire, 1994a, 1990). While Freire was not fully attuned to the political aspect of his early literacy work, he came to quickly realize the political implications and the non–neutrality of its process, leading him on a lifelong journey as a "radical political character" (da Silva & McLaren, 1993, p. 36).

Indeed, the dehumanizing mechanism that the oppressor utilized to distort the vocation of humanization during the time of Freire's early literacy work was one of exploitive control in which the oppressor turned the oppressed into things or into inanimate objects, repressively steering their thinking and action (Freire, 1990). This silencing perversely domesticates and reduces the oppressed to "a level of mere animal activity" (Spring, 1998, p. 65). Because they have been so beaten down, the process for them to rise from this subjected state is wrought with challenge.

That is, Freire argues that the oppressor can extraordinarily condition the mind of the oppressed so much so that they believe in their inferior state, their practical nothingness, making it impossible for them "to recognize the differences between themselves and, say, horses. Or if they recognize the differences, it is the advantage of the animals" (Freire, 1970, p. 4). Consequently, in order to announce the movement toward humanization, a denouncing of the dehumanization mechanism of oppression must be made (Freire, 1985). A place to begin toward that end is to make clear the distinction between the world of nature (i.e., animals) and the world of cultural beings (i.e., human beings).

The existential difference between animals and human beings is that the former are a-historical and simply "live" in the world, and the latter are cultural beings who "exist" in the world. In clarifying the distinction between live and exist, Freire (1990) points out that in the English language those two terms possess assumed connotations contrary to the origins of their etymology. That is, for Freire, *live* is the more rudimentary term, simply implying survival. *Exist*, on the other hand, connotes a sense of being and possessing the quality to be critical of the world and to participate and to meaningfully communicate in relationship with others who exist in the world (Freire, 1994b).

In that light, animals, thus, are not able to separate themselves from their activities vis–à–vis reflecting on why they do what they do. Animals simply adapt, are not capable of consciously objectifying, have no concept of yesterday or tomorrow— they merely live in the now. Here, Freire frames his thought borrowing from Marx (1995), who argues that animals simply respond to their environment as a result of physical need as opposed to thoughtful considerations. In other words, animals do not consider the world; rather, they are simply *in* the world and do not have the ability to "name" it (Freire, 1990; Freire, 1985).[12]

Conversely, human beings are conscious beings who exist, establish a relationship with the world and possess the ability to create history. However, a world that dehumanizes is a place where human beings (oppressor) forcefully strip other human beings (oppressed) from asserting their voice, i.e., naming their world. For Freire, both the oppressed and the oppressor are living in a dehumanized state; for the former they have been subjected to living in silence; for the latter, they cease to humanly exist because of their dehumanizing action (Freire, 1990; Collins, 1977). Both are in need of freedom, yet are in fear of it; for the oppressed, the fear is the actual acceptance of freedom; for the oppressor, it is fear "of losing the 'freedom' to oppress" (Freire, 1990, p. 31).

Though a complex and an often difficult–to–understand process, a critical way to move toward freedom for both parties is through dialogue. Clearly, requiring the theological virtue of hope, a deep humility, the courage to love, and a profound faith in humanity, dialogue requires a horizontal relationship (see Chapter 5) in order for reality to be recreated for both the oppressor and the oppressed (Freire, 1990). Also, in order to move from a world of actions that are dehumanizing to ones that are humanizing, human beings must not be viewed and treated as things, and all must be free to live in freedom to speak their existence. The point is that human beings, unlike animals, through their engagement in praxis (reflection and action) (see Chapter 6), possess the ability to transform their very existential reality (Freire, 1990).

The critical move toward coming from out of the shadows requires of the oppressed to ontologically recognize themselves as unfinished conscious beings, yet subjects who, in Hegel's dialectic of becoming, are situated in a historical context (Collins, 1977). That is, as subject (as opposed to object) in the unfolding process of becoming, one observes and interacts with the world while simultaneously considering cultural, historical, social, and political circumstances. Freire (1994b), acknowledging Fromm's influence, argues that the act of knowing is not something whereby the subject passively accepts or learns content that has been imposed; rather, the act of knowing is where one, through critical reflection and transforming action, behaves as subject with engagement in his/her reality in the continuous search for knowledge, ultimately becoming critically "aware of the '*raison d'être*' behind the knowing and the conditioning to which that process is subject" (p. 101).

Moving toward critical awareness thus implies a phenomenological lens whereby an examination of consciousness is essential in order to make sense of reality. However, movement toward that end is particularly difficult for individuals or groups who have lived for years under oppressive circumstances, i.e., in a state of objectification. As earlier alluded, the oppressed have been so systematically conditioned that the notion of freedom is frightening (Fromm, 1940). Moreover, their colonized state has so stunted their ability to critically think that they ultimately submit to taking on the thinking and characteristics that have been imposed on them (Memmi, 1991).

In other words, if the oppressed are not even aware of the social and economic reasons for the living and working conditions in which they find themselves, they not only accept their exploited state, but they also become convinced of their inferiority. This colonized state ultimately leads the oppressed into an emotional and mental downward spiral of death, which is acutely manifested in their inability to critically analyze and make decisions (Freire, 1994b, 1990). Freire (1990) puts it this way: "So often do they [oppressed] hear that they are good for nothing, know nothing and are incapable of learning anything—that they are sick, lazy, and unproductive—that in the end they become convinced of their own unfitness" (p. 49).

As Freire moved more intensely into his early literacy work with adult learners who lived their lives in an oppressive state, the more he began to realize the psychological, social, and political implications of his work. In short, the oppressed were "massified," meaning they were so manipulated to work and act mechanically (Freire, 1994b). Thus, talk of freedom, voice, and participation was a frightening thought, even a burden, for those who virtually lived their entire existence in a massified state. Freire (1990) puts it the following way:

> The oppressed suffer from the duality which has established itself in their innermost being. They discover that without freedom they cannot exist authentically. Yet, although they desire authentic existence, they fear it. They are at one and the same time themselves and the oppressor whose consciousness they have internalized. (p. 32)

Freire's great task was clearly to somehow challenge the consciousness that the oppressed had internalized. Certainly easier said than done, growth toward that end occurs through Freire's notion of conscientization (see Chapter 7). In brief, however, conscientization is a complex process that involves growing in critical awareness, ultimately leading to a new understanding of self, reality, and action.

A VISIONARY OF HOPE

Freire (1990) makes the critical point that his political–ethical–pedagogical philosophy is not one that would be embraced by sectarians from either the right or left simply because of its inability to escape from its "circles of certainty." In other words, "Sectarianism in any quarter is an obstacle to the emancipation of mankind [humankind]...Both types of sectarian, treating history in an equally proprietary fashion, end up without the people—which is another way of being against them" (pp. 20–21).[13] Rather, as a "radical political character," Freire (1990) argues,

> The radical, committed to human liberation, does not become the prisoner of a "circle of certainty" with which he [or she] also imprisons reality. On the contrary, the more radical he [or she] is, the more fully he [or she] enters into reality so that, knowing it better, he [or she] can better transform it. He [or she] is not afraid to confront, to listen, to see the world unveiled. He [or she] is not afraid to meet the people or to enter into dialogue with them. He [or she] does not consider himself [or herself] the proprietor of history or of men [and women], or the liberator of the oppressed; but he [or she] does commit himself, within history, to fight at their side. (pp. 23–24)

For Freire, education should not be an endeavor to domesticate, but rather one that works toward critical awareness action, which is fundamentally grounded in the theological virtue of hope. For hope is not silent, does not see reality as unchangeable, but rather sees change as possible in solidarity with those who have been victimized by dehumanizing situations and structures (for a further discussion of the concept of hope see Chapters 4 and 5).

Indeed, Freire remained unwavering in his life's work toward cultivating the betterment of humanity where ultimately oppression would cease and a culture of silence would no longer exist.[14] Influenced by the optimism of Mounier, radiated in a Franciscan love for the poor, and directed in an activism reflected in the work of Peter Maurin, Dorothy Day, and Pope Francis all of whom emphasized making visible in practice the spiritual nature of God in humanizing humanity, Freire understood the importance of a vision.

No doubt, he was familiar with the Hebrew text "Without a vision, the people perish" (Proverbs 29:18); but for Freire (1998d), he paraphrases it differently by stating, "Without a vision for tomorrow, hope is impossible" (p. 45). Freire's prophetic vision of hope saw a more just world, a more democratic society, a place that would celebrate differences, and a people who would live among each other in respect, love, and freedom.

NOTES

[1] Wherever he traversed, Maurin was fond of saying, "There is a man in France called Emmanuel Mounier. He wrote a book called The Personalist Manifesto. You should read that book" (Zwick & Zwick, 2005, p. 115).
[2] It is also worth pointing out that in drawing from the works of Albert C. Knudson (*The Philosophy of Personalism. A Study in the Metaphysics of Religion* (1927)), and Hubert E. Langan (*The Philosophy of Personalism and Its Educational Applications* (1935), De Tavernier (2009) asserts that personalism first emerged on the scene from the thought of Plato and Plotinus. And while personalism can be traced to the early Greeks, it is also true that it is linked to ancient Hindu philosophy and Confucianism (Buford, n.d.).
[3] The poem reads as follows: I Am Somebody. I Am Somebody. I May Be Poor But I Am Somebody. I May Be Young But I Am Somebody. I May Be On Welfare But I Am Somebody. I May Be Small But I Am Somebody. I May Make A Mistake But I Am Somebody. My Clothes Are Different, My Face Is Different, My Hair Is Different But I Am Somebody. I Am Black, Brown, White. I Speak A Different Language But I Must Be Respected, Protected, Never Rejected. I Am God's Child. I Am Somebody. Bringing national attention to the poem, the Reverend Jesse Jackson recited it (though his modified version) with children in chorus in 1971 at an appearance on *Sesame Street*, and later the "I am Somebody" mantra has often been heard at rallies in which Jackson speaks.
[4] Born in Grenoble, France, near the French Alps, Mounier abandoned his medical studies and sought the guidance of Jacques Chevalier, leading him to the work of Henri Bergson, Charles Péguy, and Jacques Maritain, among others (Sawchenko, 2013).
[5] Mounier (1938) further explains, "A person is a spiritual being, constituted as such by its manner of existence and independence of being; it maintains this existence by its adhesion to a hierarchy of values that it has freely adopted, assimilated, and lived by its own responsible activity and by a constant interior development; thus it unifies all its activity in freedom and by means of creative acts develops the individuality of its vocation…It is not sufficient for us to understand, we must do. Our final objective is not simply to develop in ourselves or in those about us a maximum of consciousness and sincerity, but rather to assume a maximum of responsibility and to transform a maximum of living reality…We are well aware that those who could be of help take their desire to do very seriously…It means at once fashioning myself by my acts and fashioning the reality of history" (pp. 68, 267). To be sure, the intimate link of the development of the inner life and its relationship with the community is a cornerstone of the Gospel message.
[6] As the Franciscan Richard Rohr (2013) puts it, individualism is that in which one retreats into self to find ultimate truth in an egocentric way that says, "I alone will be my reference point" (p. 2).
[7] Furthermore Mounier (1938) argues that spirituality is that deeper part of oneself, and contrary to Marxism, human civilization or culture cannot exist apart from the metaphysical. That is, "Only a program that looks beyond effort and production, a science that looks beyond utility, an art that looks

beyond agreement, and finally a personal life devoted to a spiritual reality that carries each one beyond himself — are capable of lifting the weight of a dead past and giving birth to a truly new order" (p. 7). In the end, for Mounier (1962) Christian humanism rests in Divine generosity and despite the reality of human suffering that exists and the paradoxical nature that life can be, he characterizes his perspective as that of "tragic optimism" as opposed to a pessimism that drives some humanist thought.

[8] Cunningham (1987) asserts that it was between the 14th–16th century, as a response or a turning away from medieval scholasticism, in which originally a philosophy of humanism first emerged as the "New Learning" in an effort to rediscover the ancient writings of the ancient Greek and Roman texts through the writings of Petrarch, Lorenzo Valla, Erasmus, Thomas More, and others

[9] The English translation of that book is titled *The Spoil of the Violent*, and in the text Mounier (1955) argues that Christianity must move from a conservative, and even bourgeois, illusionary way of thinking and doing to a more heroic and bold Christianity that is propelled by a spirit of freedom and grace in an authentic love for God and others.

[10] Freire's belief system, thusly, was not driven by a fatalistic perspective whereby if something may not have gone his way or if something was going wrong (for example, the hunger crises he faced as a child), he would have reduced the failure or misfortunate as simply one that was God's will or a test of faith from God (Freire, 1996). Particularly in light of the cultural context of his era, the latter point is no small matter because for many during that time (and remnants of this thinking still exists today), misfortunate and poverty were somehow predetermined, as if a part of God's grand plan and test. And the "encouragement" from the religious establishment was that one should simply "offer" their misery up to God and their reward would come soon enough in the afterlife, in heaven. This type of thinking, as discussed in Chapter 4, is rooted in a colonial legacy or in what Freire characterizes as the traditionalist church, which in its worst sense is the missionary church that simply focused on "winning" souls, often through masochistic threats, emphasizing the more one suffers, the more one is purified in achieving eternal salvation (Freire, 1985).

[11] Making the clear distinction between the two, Roberts (2000) states,

> Humanization and dehumanization are both concrete possibilities for human beings, but only humanization is an ontological and historical vocation. The vocation of becoming more fully human is what defines us as human beings; it is the *essence* of being human. Humanization is an historical, as well as ontological, vocation because it calls us to act (on the basis of critical reflection) in the objective world of lived social relations. Dehumanization represents a distortion of this vocation. (p. 45)

In that light, the dehumanizing mechanism that the oppressor utilized to distort the vocation of humanization during the time of Freire's early literacy work was one of exploitive control in which the oppressor turned the oppressed into things or into inanimate objects, repressively steering their thinking and action (Freire, 1990). While Freire's early work had as its particular concentration on class oppression, it was not at the expense that he was mindful of other modes of oppression. In later work, he was more specific regarding oppressive systems that, for example, impacted the lives of women and people of color (Roberts, 2000; Freire & Macedo, 1993).

[12] Albeit it is worth mentioning that there is a growing body of research that is critically exploring the "consciousness" or "thinking" level of some species of animals and their capacity to reason.

[13] As mentioned Chapter 5, but bears repeating, a parallel to Freire's assertion is exemplified by Oscar Romero, the martyred Salvadoran Archbishop, when he took what Rohr (1987) describes as the naked position of the gospel—one that is not pleasing to the political left or right. Rather, Romero's position was one to transparently illuminate reality and proclaim a God of love and justice. Romero (1979) earnestly declares:

> It's amusing: This week I received accusations from both extremes—from the extreme right, that I am a communist; from the extreme left, that I am joining the right. I am not with the right or with the left. I am trying to be faithful to the word that the Lord bids me preach, to the message that cannot change, which tells both sides the good they do and the injustices they commit. (p. 163)

[14] As a result of colonization, a closed society was established in Brazil (and other Latin American countries), represented by a way of governing that was rigid, hierarchical, and one that cultivated a "culture of silence." In other words, the Portuguese invaders advanced a way of operating that was necrophilic, which means treating people as objects, without voice and choice, and perpetrating overwhelming control, by any means necessary (Freire, 1990). Here, Freire (1990, 1970) draws from Fromm's *The Heart of Man* (1968), where he discusses the different orientations between "biophilic" and "necrophilic." The former is action toward humanization and the latter toward dehumanization. In short, the dehumanizing action of the dominators consequently configured a society of dependence. So, what began with the conquest of Brazil in its creation of a closed society and its violent efforts to establish a culture of silence (or a society of silence) has been one in which the remnants were clearly manifested during the time Freire embarked on his literacy work. And despite some progress, contemporary Brazil is largely an economically dependent society in which the ideology of capitalism perpetuates the furthering of the dominant group, while at the same time fostering the status quo. Stated another way, vestiges of a patrimonial order continue to operate in Brazil in which relatively only a small group of elites possesses the most power, where possession of the land and major business enterprises has been principally owned by the dominant group while the majority of the masses has been generationally left out with little opportunity to economically move forward and largely remain in poverty and subjected to poorly functioning schools (Roett, 1972; Freire, 1996, 2004).

REFERENCES

Andreola, B. A. (2004). Letter to Paulo Freire. In P. Freire (Ed.), *Pedagogy of indignation* (pp. XXXIII–XLV). Boulder, CO: Paradigm Publishers.

Buber, M. (1958). *I and thou* (2nd ed.). New York, NY: Scribner.

Buford, T. O. (n.d.). Personalism. *Internet Encyclopedia of Philosophy: A Peer-Reviewed Academic Resource.* Retrieved from http://www.iep.utm.edu/personal/

Collins, D. E.. (1977). *Paulo Freire: His life, works and thought.* New York, NY: Paulist Press.

Cunningham, L. S. (1987). Humanism. In J. A. Komonchak, M. Collins, & D. A. Lane (Eds.), *The new dictionary of theology* (pp. 498–500). Collegeville, MN: The Liturgical Press.

da Silva, T. T., & McLaren, P. (1993). Knowledge under siege: The Brazilian debate. In P. McLaren & P. Leonard (Eds.), *Paulo Freire: A critical encounter* (pp. 36–46). New York, NY: Routledge.

Day, D. (1945, September). Peter the materialist. *The Catholic Worker*, 6. Retrieved from http://www.catholicworker.org/dorothyday/articles/152.html

De Tavernier, J. (2009). The historical roots of personalism: From Renouvier's le personnalisme, Mounier's manifeste au service du personnalisme and Maritain's humanisme intégral to Janssens' personne et société. *Ethical Perspectives, 16*(3), 361–392.

Edwords, F. (n.d.). What is humanism. *American Humanist Association.* Retrieved from http://americanhumanist.org/Humanism/What_is_Humanism

Elias, J. L. (1994). *Paulo Freire: Pedagogue of liberation.* Malabar, FL: Kreiger Publishing Company.

Eneau, J. (2008). From autonomy to reciprocity, or vice versa? French personalism's contribution to a new perspective on self–directed learning. *Adult Education Quarterly, 58*(3), 229–248.

Fraser, J. W. (1997). *Love and history in the work of Paulo Freire.* In P. Freire, J. W. Fraser, D. Macedo, T. McKinnon, & W. T. Stokes (Eds.), *Mentoring the mentor: A critical dialogue with Paulo Freire* (pp. 175–199). New York, NY: Peter Lang.

Freire, P. (1970). *Cultural action: A dialectic analysis.* Centro Intercultural de Documentacion (CIDOC) Cuaderno No. 1004. APDO. 479 Cuernavaca, Mexico.

Freire, P. (1985). *The politics of education: Culture, power, and liberation.* New York, NY: Bergin & Garvey.

Freire, P. (1990). *Pedagogy of the oppressed.* New York, NY: Continuum.

Freire, P. (1994a). *Pedagogy of hope: Reliving pedagogy of the oppressed* (R. R. Barr, Trans.). New York, NY: Continuum.

Freire, P. (1994b). *Education for critical consciousness.* New York, NY: Continuum.

Freire, P. (1996). *Letters to Cristina: Reflections on my life and work* (D. Macedo, Q. Macedo, & A. Oliveira, Trans.). New York, NY: Routledge.

Freire, P. (1997). A response. In P. Freire, J. W. Fraser, D. Macedo, T. McKinnon, & W. T. Stokes (Eds.), *Mentoring the mentor: A critical dialogue with Paulo Freire* (pp. 303–329). New York, NY: Peter Lang.

Freire, P. (1998d). *Pedagogy of the heart*. New York, NY: Continuum.

Freire, P. (2004). *Pedagogy of indignation*. Boulder, CO: Paradigm Publishers.

Freire, P., & Macedo, D. (1993). A dialogue with Paulo Freire. In P. McLaren & P. Leonard (Eds.), *Paulo Freire: A critical encounter* (pp. 169–176). London, England: Routledge.

Fromm, E. (1940). *Escape from freedom*. New York, NY: Holt, Rinehart and Winston.

Fromm, E. (1968). *The heart of man: Its genius for good and evil*. New York, NY: Harper and Row.

Inglis, W. B. (1959). Personalism, analysis, and education. *International Review of Education, 5*(4), 383–399.

Kirylo, J. D. (Ed.). (2013). *A critical pedagogy of resistance: 34 pedagogues we need to know*. Rotterdam, The Netherlands: Sense Publishers.

Knudson, A. C. (1969/1927). *The philosophy of personalism. A study in the metaphysics of religion*. New York-Cincinnati: Abingdon (Reprinted, New York: Kraus Reprint).

Koterski, J. W. (2012). Personalism. *First Principles: ISI Web Journal*. Retrieved from http://www.firstprinciplesjournal.com/print.aspx?article=332&loc=b&type=cbbp

Langan, H. E. (1935). *The philosophy of personalism and its educational applications* (Ph.D. dissertation). The Catholic University of America, Washington, DC.

Marx, K. (1995). *Capital* (An abridged edition, D. McLellan, Ed.). Oxford, CT: Oxford University Press.

Memmi, A. (1991). *The colonizer and the colonized* (Expanded edition). Boston, MA: Beacon Press.

Mounier, E. (1938). *A personalist manifesto* (Translated from the French by monks of St. John's). London: Longmans, Green and Co.

Mounier, E. (1952). *Personalism*. London, England: Routledge & Kegan Paul, LTD. (First published in France, 1950).

Mounier, E. (1955). *The spoil of the violent* (K. Watson, Trans.). London: The Harvill Press.

Mounier, E. (1962). *Be not afraid: A denunciation of despair*. New York, NY: Sheed and Ward.

Mounier, E. (1995, March). Emmanuel Mounier and personalism. *Houston Catholic Worker, XV*(2). Retrieved from http://cjd.org/1995/03/01/emmanuel-mounier-and-personalism/

Roberts, P. (2000). *Education, literacy, and humanization: Exploring the work of Paulo Freire*. Westport, CT: Bergin & Garvey.

Roett, R. (1972). *Brazil: Politics in a patrimonial society*. Boston, MA: Allyn and Bacon, Inc.

Rohr, R. (1987). *Beyond our cultural biases: Siding with the cosmic Christ*. Cincinnati, OH: St. Anthony Messenger Tapes.

Rohr, R. (2013). *Immortal diamond: The search for our true self*. San Francisco, CA: Josey-Bass (A Wiley Imprint).

Sawchenko, L. D. (2013). *The concept of person: The contribution of Gabriel Marcel and Emmanuel Mounier to the philosophy of Paul Ricoeur* (Master of Arts Thesis). Department of Religious Studies, Calgary, Alberta.

Spring, J. (1998). *A primer of libertarian education*. Buffalo, NY: Black Rose Books.

Williams, T. D., & Bengtsson, J. O. (2016). Personalism. In E. N. Zalta (Ed.), *The Stanford encyclopedia of philosophy*. Retrieved from http://plato.stanford.edu/archives/sum2016/entries/personalism.

Zwick, M., & Zwick, L. (2005). *The Catholic Worker movement: Intellectual and spiritual origins* (Reprinted p. 115, from *The Catholic Worker*, April, 1950). New York, NY & Mahwah, NJ: Paulist Press.

HOPE, HISTORY AND UTOPIA

INTRODUCTION

In 2010 I (Drick) attended the U.S. Social Forum in Detroit, a gathering of 15 thousand community organizers, popular educators, labor organizers, and social justice advocates from across the United States. In a surprising but profound way, I was struck by the deeply spiritual nature of the proceedings. People spoke of their commitment to social justice and concern for the victims of abusive corporate and government policies. They sang songs, many of which were gospel songs with the words slightly altered. Several participants spoke of their commitment to each other and to the "movement" in personal terms that reiterated deep convictions. In private conversations, I learned that many of the participants were strengthened by a sense of purpose that came from their religious faith, be it Jewish, Christian, Muslim or undefined.

Through it all, I was reminded that some of the most effective activists for social change, such as Martin Luther King Jr., Stephen Biko, Mohandas Gandhi, Malcolm X, and Dorothy Day, were also individuals of deep spiritual commitment—in the same way Paulo Freire, whose writings have influenced educators, activists, and students around the world, operated out of a deep sense of faith. In fact, at the heart of Freire's spirituality is his unwavering hope that justice would one day prevail.

Denis Collins (1977) characterizes Freire this way:

> How is one to account for the optimism of Paulo Freire? ... Freire's life and work as an educator is optimistic in spite of poverty, imprisonment and exile.... On a planet where more than half the people go hungry every day because nations are incapable of feeding all their citizens, where we cannot agree that every being has a right to eat, Paulo Freire toils to help men and women overcome their sense of powerlessness to act on their own behalf. (p. 3)

Despite his own personal suffering and the overwhelming inequities he encountered in his work around the world, Freire maintained a positive outlook on the course of human history and saw himself as a person of hope. He wrote, "Above all my difference lies in my critical, in no-way-naïve optimism and the hope that encourages me and that does not exist for the fatalistic" (Freire, 1997, p. 44).

While rooted in his Roman Catholic faith, Freire's understanding of hope originated from several places. From Marxism he gained a paradigm for understanding the dynamics of human history. From the Personalism of Emmanuel Mounier he gained a humanizing perspective on the struggle for liberation.[1] The philosophical concept of Utopia provided an image toward which his concept of hope could focus. After making a brief comment about Personalism, we will look more fully at the impact of Marxism and the concept of Utopia on Freire's ideas about hope. We will then look specifically at the ways in which Freire articulated and practiced that hope. For Freire hope was not simply a concept, but what he called an "ontological need" and "an existential; concrete imperative" that guided and drove his life and work (Freire, 1992, p. 8).

PERSONALISM

As was noted in Chapter 1, Freire re-embraced his Roman Catholic faith that he had briefly abandoned in his adolescence when he entered college. Key to that change in perspective were the writings of Catholic humanist philosophers such as Emmanuel Mounier (Elias, 1994). A starting point for understanding the theological underpinnings of Freire's views on hope and utopia can be found in the Personalist philosophy developed by Mounier, which is fully explored in Chapter 3.

In addition to Mounier's impact on Freire's view of humanization, many of the themes found in Mounier's writings on the role of God in human history are also found in Freire (Collins, 1977). For instance, Mounier believed that the shape and destination of history are not predetermined, but rather are created by human beings working as co-creators with God in the making of history. Central for Mounier is the idea that Christianity is a religion of Incarnation. The transcendent (God) is incarnated in the men and women who are living and working in history. Because of their particular orientation toward transcendent values, Christians seek to direct history in accordance with those Christian values, and are on the watch for any deviation from those values. For Mounier (1950) this striving was primarily a communal rather than individual endeavor, whereby the Christian community acts as a guard against religious subjectivism. As we shall see these same themes can be found in Freire when he speaks of hope and the role of the person in relationship to God shaping the course of history.

UTOPIA

At the heart of Freire's view of history in the struggle for liberation and the humanization of persons is the concept of Utopia, which has a long and varied history in literature and social thought. At its heart "Utopia is about how we would live and what kind of world we would live in if we could do just that" (Levitas, 2010, p. 19). The word "utopia" literally means "no place" and for some writers, such as Thomas More, utopia was a concept that was considered an impractical goal. Others, such as Moritz Kaufmann, while seeing the attainment of utopia as impossible, nonetheless saw that it served the positive role of causing people to explore the possibilities and roles of working toward an ideal society. For him this ideal society took the form of a utopian socialist state; in essence socialism for Kaufmann was both the means and the end of the utopian quest. Lewis Mumford went further and drew a distinction between utopias of escape and utopias of reconstruction. The utopias of escape are ultimately destructive to the good of society because they draw people away from civic life into fanciful pursuits of personal fulfillment. Utopias of reconstruction, on the other hand, are visions of an ideal community that encourage the development of new habits, fresh values, and a more socially conducive social structure (Levitas, 2010).

Contrary to these thinkers, Marx and Engels rejected utopia not so much because of its form, but because its content was shaped around a bourgeois ideal that did not take into account the inequities created by industrialization and the concentration of wealth, capital, and power. Furthermore, unlike many utopian thinkers who saw humanity evolving progressively toward the utopian ideal, Marx and Engels did not believe any form of an improved society could come about without a process of protracted struggle between the workers and the owners of the means of production, the bourgeoisie and the proletariat, the oppressed and the oppressors. Thus, they rejected utopia not so much for its ideal, but for the romanticized way it was believed to come into being (Levitas, 2010).

Negley and Patrick counter these criticisms by noting that utopia emanates from the highest aspirations that people can have, the possibility of dreaming of a better world. From their perspective, human progress flows from this dream of something better. As Levitas (2010) in her overview of these different perspectives on utopia states: "The main function identified for utopia is as an ideal which, while strictly speaking impossible to realize, nevertheless (in some unspecified way) helps history to unfold in a positive direction" (p. 39).

However, Gutiérrez (2015) is not content to allow utopia to remain an unattainable dream. Gutiérrez uses utopia as a concept to challenge the current state of the social order so as to break open a new reality for the poor. While Gutiérrez (1971) recognizes that for More utopia refers to something illusory and unrealistic, he chooses instead to see utopia has having the "quality of being subversive and a driving force of history" (p. 232). Utopia suggests that the current order must be repudiated for its dehumanizing quality, while at the same time pointing to a new order characterized by humanizing values, equity and social justice. Rather than being "an evasion of reality," belief in utopia "must necessarily lead to a commitment to support the emergence of a new social consciousness and new relationships among people" (p. 234). He even goes so far as to say that utopia "constitutes the essence of [science's] creativity and dynamism" (p. 234). Utopia constitutes a call to action that arises from faith in a God of liberation and the need for concrete political action. Instead of the fancies of dreamers, for Gutiérrez utopia radicalizes the commitment of individuals and communities in the present to work toward the establishment of an equitable and just society.

Freire integrated the more reconstructionist view of utopia of Mumford with the radicalizing vision of Gutiérrez. From Freire's perspective, utopia was not some far off, never-to-be-seen reality, but a vision of a free and just society that draws the oppressed from their fatalism into liberating action. He characterized utopia as "the aspiration for the radical changes in society in such areas as economics, human relationships, property, the right to employment, to land, to education and to health" (Freire, 1998, p. 6). Furthermore, utopia results from the dismantling of the oppressive forces and structures that denied such basic human rights to certain citizens. He would agree with Kowalski who says "utopia is a tool of action upon reality and of planning social action" (quoted in Elias, 1994, p. 58). For Freire utopia was not necessarily a reality that would soon be achieved, but rather a long-range vision, which motivated one to act.

A key to understanding his concept of utopia was the power of imagination. Freire described his commitment to utopia as "a dialectical relationship between denouncing the present and announcing the future. To anticipate tomorrow by dreaming today" (Shor & Freire, 1987, p. 187). Elsewhere he writes: "There is no change without dream, as there is no dream without hope" (Freire, 1992, p. 91). Referring to Freire's perspective, Gutiérrez (1971) writes "If utopia does not lead to action in the present, it is an evasion of reality" (p. 234). Thus, for Freire a proper understanding of utopia required one to maintain a clear balance between the imagined and hoped-for future, and the critical analysis and concrete action that was needed to achieve that future.

MARXISM

While not sharing Marx's critique of the concept of utopia as bourgeois, Freire did draw significantly from Marx for his understanding of the dynamics of human history and social change, which in Freire's terms was to "read the world" (Freire & Macedo, 1987). When he began his literacy work, Freire operated out of the philosophy of Christian humanism characteristic of the Catholic Action movement and only later embraced Marxist language to describe his experiences and his educational philosophy. Freire described the process this way:

> When I was a young man, I went to the people, to the workers, the peasants, motivated, really, by my Christian faith … When I arrived with the people – the misery, the concreteness, you know! … The obstacles of this reality sent me – to Marx. I started reading and studying. It was beautiful because I found in Marx a lot of the things the people had told me – without being literate. Marx was a genius. (quoted in Elias, 1994, p. 42)

In essence Freire's faith and the reality of the situation led him to Marx and helped make sense of a desperate and complex situation.

Actually, Freire was probably more influenced by Marxist and neo-Marxist thinkers such as Mounier, Mao Tse-Tung, Che Guevara, and Gramsci, than the writings of Marx himself (Roberts, 1998). Since, from Freire's perspective, educators can never be politically neutral, it is therefore important for them to have a worldview and perspective from which they do their pedagogical work

(Freire, 1992; Aronowitz, 1998). The language and thought forms of Marx provided that perspective, and therefore are evident throughout Freire's writing (Freire & Macedo, 2000).

Perhaps most evident to even the casual reader of Freire is the influence of Marx's perspective on class struggle. Freire's reflections on education start from the perspective of the "wretched of the earth, the excluded" (Freire, 1998, p. 220). Like Marx, Freire emphasized the inherent contradiction between oppressors and oppressed in the social world, a dialectic that Marx believed leads to class struggle and revolutionary social change (Roberts, 2000).

A theme that runs throughout Freire's writings is an analysis of oppression and its impact on both oppressor and oppressed (Elias, 1994). In *Pedagogy of the Oppressed* Freire (1993) details the impact that the experience of oppression has on the thinking and action of the poor. He then proceeds to describe how the oppressed and oppressor exist in a dialectically destructive relationship that can only be resolved through significant social change. Like Marx, Freire saw that knowledge was a by-product of one's social and political circumstances. Oppressive and impoverished social circumstances condition people to a passive acceptance of reality and a fatalism regarding the possibility of change. The role of the educator is to help oppressed persons critically reflect on those circumstances and thereby initiate a process of social change (Freire, 1985). Unlike Marx, but like Marxists such as Mao and Che Guevara, Freire believed that engaging persons in dialogue was key to this consciousness raising process (Elias, 1994).

Marxist thought also influenced Freire's perspective on the progress of human history. Like Marx, Freire had tremendous faith in the potential of human beings to change the course of history. Elias (1994) writes that Freire believed, "Humans know the world, construct the world, and are able to change the world" (p. 54). He believed the oppressed were caught up in a situation that could be transformed from oppression to liberation through critical reflection and political action. While he often spoke of this liberation process in general terms, he saw that the particular circumstances of a given socio-political situation caused that process to express itself in a variety of ways (Freire & Macedo, 2000). He believed that history could move toward a Marxist vision of a classless society. However, in Freire's view this progress is not inevitable. Rather, history presents people with an opportunity for progressive change, and the oppressed must struggle for justice to change the balance of power and grasp the possibility of true political freedom (Freire, 1992).

Freire also shared Marx's critique of organized religion as an "opiate of the masses." Though he came to a different understanding of the church's role in social change (discussed below), he recognized that often organized religion encourages the poor to accept their state and to look to the afterlife for their reward. Religion also entices people to engage in various forms of magical thinking that keeps them from confronting the realities that are oppressing them. In that way he believed the church contributed to the fatalistic mentality exhibited by many of the peasants he encountered (Freire, 1972, 1985; Elias 1994).

Related to Freire's commitment to revolution was his somewhat controversial view on the place of violence in the revolutionary process. Marx saw violence as an inevitable consequence of class struggle. Freire shared that view, but was less accepting of its necessity. Freire's second wife, Nita, states that he was never an advocate of violence or armed struggle (Freire & Macedo, 2000). McLaren (2000) distinguishes Freire's revolutionary practice from that of Che Guevara in that Freire saw violence as unfortunate but inevitable, whereas Che believed one must use violence in the revolutionary struggle. Freire saw that oppression often leads to a process that involves violent struggle. However, he insisted that violence is never initiated by the oppressed, but rather by the oppressors. He wrote, "Force is not used by those who have become weak under the preponderance of the strong, but by the strong who have emasculated them" (Freire, 1993, p. 41). In other words, revolutionary change often leads to violence as a reaction to the violence of the oppressor.

Freire did not advocate "inciting rebellion," but rather placed great emphasis on the importance of love, which leads people to dialogue. He wrote, "Dialogue cannot exist, however, in the absence of profound love for the world and for people. The naming of the world, which is an act of creation and re-creation is not possible if it is not infused with love" (1970/1992, p. 77). Freire believed that love involves a concern for the Other, and leads to liberating action. Love is the "oxygen of revolution", the sustaining power for those involved in revolutionary struggle. In this sense Freire departs from Marx, but embraces the attitude of Che Guevara, whose Marxist revolutionary philosophy was also centered in a profound love for people (McLaren, 2000).[2]

Thus, Freire's adaptation of Marxist thought was complicated. While he did not fully embrace Marx's solution to the problem of oppression, he nonetheless found Marxist categories and concepts helpful in communicating a perspective on the nature of oppression and the need for revolutionary change. Freire was impressed by Marx's concern for the poor and found his philosophy to be a helpful tool for analyzing society, which in turn provided a framework for his educational philosophy. However, he neither accepted Marx's determinism nor his advocacy of violence as the means to true liberation.

FREIRE'S THEOLOGY OF HOPE AND HISTORY

With these thoughts as background, let us look at how Freire conceived of and practiced hope in his educational and political work. In the opening pages of *Pedagogy of Hope*, Freire (1992) outlines the essential nature of hope in human existence. He recounts being ridiculed by a colleague for writing a book on hope in the "shameless hellhole of corruption" of Brazil. Yet even in the cynicism and despair characterizing that statement, he recognizes the rudiments of hope. For Freire hope is not an option but "an ontological need" and a "concrete imperative;" that is, hope is not something that descends upon one, but a choice one makes in his/her approach to the world; hope is the "untested feasibility," and our basic human nature drives us to seek after it. However, hope must also be anchored in one's actions, if the object of one's hope is to be realized; yet without hope, those actions may never be initiated. So he wrote *Pedagogy of Hope* "in rage and love, without which there is no hope" (p. 8).

His views regarding history and social change sprang from a clear, though not fully articulated, theological foundation. Growing out of the influence of Personalism, Freire (1972b) believed "[t]heology has to take its starting point from anthropology." In a letter to a friend, Freire (1972b) articulated his views on God's role in history. He criticized those who assumed that God's involvement in history was a reason for an attitude of passive waiting. By contrast Freire believed that salvation (and liberation) has to be "achieved." That is, one has to actively work for and pursue the justice one hopes for. To wait passively upon God to act in some transcendent way is to make oneself "an accomplice of injustice, of un-love, of the exploitation of men [sic] in the world."

In a letter to a theology student, Freire (1972a) outlines his theology of hope. He begins by stating that Christians cannot bring about change in people's lives without also addressing the conditions of the world in which they live. He writes, "it is idle to talk of changing man [sic] without changing also the concrete circumstances he lives in: transforming them will transform him too—not automatically, of course, but quite certainly" (para 2).

Central to the actions Christians take is their response to the Word of God. From the context of his writing, it appears that for Freire the Word of God was the whole of the Christian message collectively found in the Bible, the doctrines of the church, preaching, and the personal sharing of the gospel message. Freire wrote that in order to hear the Word of God one must be willing to commit oneself to the work of liberating those who are oppressed and to actually engage in that "transforming activity". He put it this way,

> In the final analysis, the Word of God is inviting me to re-create the world, not for my brothers' domination, but for their liberation. I am not really able to hear that Word, then, unless I am fired up to live it fully. Listening to the Word of God does not mean acting like empty vessels waiting to be filled with that Word. The Word of God is not some content to be poured into us as if we were mere static recipients for it. And because it saves, that Word also liberates, but men [sic] have to accept it historically. They must make themselves subjects, agents of their salvation and liberation. (1972a, p. 7)

Thus, one can see that for Freire, truly hearing the Word of God moves one to actively work against oppression and for liberation.

Because working for liberation was at the heart of hearing the Word of God, Freire believed that only those who were oppressed could hear the Word of God and be energized by it. Those who were not oppressed needed to give up their privileged lifestyle and perspective and steep themselves in the lives of the oppressed. Freire called this repudiation of privilege an "Easter experience" and said that it involved "repudiating the power structures, the establishments that represent the world of domination. It means siding with the oppressed, with the condemned of the earth, in a posture of authentic love that cannot possibly straddle both camps" (1972b).[3]

THE PROPHETIC ROLE OF THE CHURCH

This theological perspective put him at odds with the Roman Catholic Church of his day. Freire took a critical stance toward the church. He described his views in two similar treatises on the church (Freire, 1985). In speaking of the church, he did not speak of the church in some abstract or ideal sense, but rather the church as he had observed it acting and responding to the needs of the poor of Latin America. He rejected the notion that the church could be neutral in relation to the course of history or political action. To do so was to reinforce the position of the dominant, oppressing classes.

In particular, he criticized two different expressions of the church, which he called the Traditionalist Church and the Modernizing Church (Freire, 1985). The Traditionalist Church actively supports the status quo, and also condemns as sinners those who would seek to change the status quo. The leaders of the Traditionalist Church only hear the voices of the dominant class and condemn the poor masses as spiritually inferior. The Modernizing Church recognizes the vast disparity between the wealthy and the poor, but still does not work for social change. Rather, the Modernizing Church seeks to help those who are poor and undereducated gain the skills, knowledge, and competencies to compete effectively in the world as it is. The Modernizing Church sides with the poor, but only so far as it can help them climb out of their dire straits. At no point does the Modernizing Church question or critique the political, social and economic conditions that create that disparity.

In Freire's view the only true role for the church is the prophetic role. The Prophetic Church rejects the otherworldliness and "halfway measures" of most established churches, and instead works for the social and spiritual liberation of oppressed people. The Prophetic Church takes a critical stance toward existing socio-political structures and engages in an ongoing process of challenging the status quo on behalf of the poor and oppressed. The role of the Prophetic Church is to be "an instrument of transformative action" and societal change. In contrast to Christians in Traditionalist and Modernizing churches, Christians in the Prophetic Church have consciously sided with the poor and experience the suffering of the poor as a concrete reality rather than an abstract concept. As a result, they are moved to work for social and political change and have become committed to changing the structures that create the oppression experienced by the poor and powerless (Freire, 1985).

DENUNCIATION, ANNUNCIATION AND ACTION

The work of the prophet and the prophetic church is captured in the concepts of denunciation and annunciation. He contended that a utopian vision created a dialectical tension between the present and the future, which in turn moved both the oppressed person and the non-oppressed ally to action. This dialectic is best understood in his assertion that the educators and activists must be engaged in the practice of denunciation and annunciation. First, the utopian vision requires one to denounce the unjust and dehumanizing structures currently oppressing people. Second, the utopian vision moves one to announce that a just and humanizing structure is possible. The announcement is itself the "announcement of a project," a call to action, and a commitment to be engaged in an ongoing process of socio-political transformation. By definition the announcement of utopia is meaningless unless accompanied by the commitment to action. This process of changed perception leads to a vision of utopia, which in turn leads to commitment, which then leads to action. Both dynamics of denunciation and annunciation must be present for hope to arise. He writes, "It is necessary to go beyond rebellious attitudes to a more radically critical and revolutionary position, which is in fact a position not simply denouncing injustice but of announcing a new utopia" (Freire, 1998, p. 74)

Gutiérrez (1971) writes, "According to Freire, between the denunciation and the annunciation is the time for building, the historical praxis" (p. 234). Speaking personally, Freire (1997) wrote, "I cannot permit myself to be a mere spectator. On the contrary, I must demand my place in the process of change" (p. 129). He further pointed out that such involvement in the liberating work of history was difficult and immersed one in "the dramatic tension between the past and future, death and life, being and non-being" (p. 129). Near the end of his life, reflecting on his career, Freire said that his understanding of God and history did not excuse him from being involved, but rather pushed him to work for substantive social change. His faith perspective did not allow him to tolerate or excuse discrimination or exploitation of any kind (Freire, 1997). Like his educational philosophy, Freire's theological views were not abstract reflections of a distant observer, but rather were forged on the anvil of his lifelong work and activism with and on behalf of the poor and the illiterate.

Schipani (1998) characterizes Freire as a "millenialist," by which he means that Freire saw revelation as an ongoing process with the goal of God's action being the ordering of a just society for all people. Freire did not look for God to act outside of or beyond historical circumstances, but solely within them. Weiler (1996) says that from Freire's perspective the end of history is the result of human choices and not a matter of fate or destiny that humans can only observe and accept. As Freire (1998) said late in his life, "I insist that history is possibility and not determinism…It is impossible to understand history as possibility if we do not recognize human beings as beings who make free decisions" (p. 37). God presents the possibility, but human beings must act to make the possibility reality.

HOPE AND PERSONAL FAITH

Freire (1997) tells the story of a conversation he had with two homeless people in San Francisco. As the homeless individuals spoke of their daily struggles living on the streets, and how trapped they felt by their situation, Freire commented that the "conversation was interspersed with hopelessness throughout" (p. 101). He saw in their eyes the same despair he had witnessed in the eyes of the poor of Sao Paulo. Instead of sharing their cynicism or being drawn down by their despair, he noted that if he resigned himself to the idea that the suffering of these two homeless individuals was irreversible, "I would be betraying the desperate in the world" (p. 101). It is as if he saw that one of his roles was to inject hope where hopelessness seemed to reign. He went on to say that his faith in God was inextricably bound up in working to overcome the reality of oppression and suffering and working toward "a less ugly society, one that is less evil and more humane" (p. 104). While he recognized that some social justice progressives were motivated to work against injustice without relying on a spiritual or religious faith, for him his faith in God was essential to the hope that motivated him throughout his life.

Freire (1997) tells another story about a conversation with a Brazilian friend regarding some troubling political events in their native country. The friend admitted he came to Freire to be encouraged by his capacity for hope in the face of the disappointing events, and went away with his spirits lifted. However, upon reflection, Freire admitted "What he may not have known is that I needed him as much as he needed me." He concluded: "The struggle for hope is permanent, and it becomes intensified when one realizes it is not a solitary struggle" (p. 106).

These two personal anecdotes illustrate that for Freire hope was both rooted in the concrete struggles of the daily life of people, and drew upon a higher vision illuminated and encouraged by his faith in God. The struggle to live in hope is at one level deeply personal and solitary, and yet at its heart is also shared in community with others. As Webb (2011) writes, "the objective of hope is a shared utopian dream" (p. 334). Moreover, that hope is radical in that it moves one to act in defiance and in spite of an oppressive reality to seek after the "untested feasibility" of one's current situation (p. 335). Freire recognized that the positive future for which he worked was not a given, but was reached through concerted, collaborative action motivated by hope. As he wrote "…the future we dream is not inexorable. We have to make it, produce it, else it will not come in the form that we more or less wish it to… [The future is] a project, a dream for which we struggle" (1992, p. 101).

NOTES

[1] For a fuller discussion on Personalism, see Chapter 3.
[2] For a fuller discussion of Freire's concept of love, see Chapter 5.
[3] For a fuller discussion on the Easter Experience, see Chapter 2.

REFERENCES

Arnowitz, S. (1998). Introduction. In P. Freire (Ed.), *Pedagogy of freedom: Ethics, democracy and civic courage* (P. Clarke, Trans.). Lanham, MD: Rowman & Littlefield Publishers, Inc.
Collins, D. (1977). *Paulo Freire: His life, works, and thought.* New York, NY: Paulist Press.

Elias, J. (1994). *Paulo Freire: Pedagogue of liberation*. Malabar, FL: Krieger Publishing.

Freire, A., & Macedo, D. (Eds.). (2000). *The Paulo Freire reader*. New York, NY: Continuum.

Freire, P. (1972a). Letter to a young theology student. *LADOC 2.29a*, 11–12.

Freire, P. (1972b). The third world and theology. *LADOC 2.29a*, 13–15.

Freire, P. (1985). *The politics of education*. South Hadley, MA: Bergin & Garvey.

Freire, P. (1992). *Pedagogy of hope: Reliving the pedagogy of the oppressed*. New York, NY: Continuum.

Freire, P. (1993). *Pedagogy of the oppressed, 30th anniversary edition* (M. B. Ramos, Trans.). New York, NY: Continuum.

Freire, P. (1997). *Pedagogy of the heart* (D. Macedo & A. Oliveira, Trans.). New York, NY: Continuum International Publishing.

Freire, P. (1998). *Pedagogy of freedom: Ethics, democracy and civic courage* (P. Clarke, Trans.). Lanham, MD: Rowman & Littlefield Publishers, Inc.

Freire, P., & Macedo, D. (1987). *Literacy: Reading the word and the world*. New York, NY: Bergin & Garvey.

Gutiérrez, G. (1973). *A theology of liberation: History, politics and salvation* (Sr. C. Inda & J. Eagleson, Trans.). Maryknoll, NY: Orbis Books.

Gutiérrez, G. (2015). Where will the poor sleep? In G. Gutiérrez & G. L. Müller (Eds.), *On the side of the poor: The theology of liberation* (R. A. Krieg & J. B. Nickoloff, Trans., pp. 83–133). New York, NY: Orbis Books.

Levitas, R. (2010). *The concept of utopia*. Oxford: Peter Lang.

McLaren, P. (2000). *Che Guevara, Paulo Freire, and the pedagogy of revolution*. Lanham, MD: Rowman & Littlefield.

Mounier, E. (1950). *Personalism* (C. Rowland, Trans.). London: Routledge & Kegan Paul Ltd.

Roberts, P. (1998). Knowledge, dialogue and humanization: The moral philosophy of Paulo Freire. *Journal of Educational Thought, 32*(2), 95–117.

Roberts, P. (2000). *Education, literacy and humanization: Exploring the work of Paulo Freire*. Westport, CT: Bergin & Garvey.

Schipani, D. (1988). *Religious education encounters liberation theology*. Birmingham, AL: Religious Education Press.

Shor, I., & Freire, P. (1987). *A pedagogy for liberation: Dialogues on transforming education*. Westport, CT: Bergin & Garvey.

Webb, D. (2011). Paulo Freire and "the need for a kind of education in hope." *Cambridge Journal of Education, 40*(4), 327–339.

Weiler, K. (1996). Myths of Paulo Freire. *Educational Theory, 46*(3), 353–371.

CHAPTER 5

GROUNDED IN THE WELL OF LOVE

So faith, hope, love remain, these three; but the greatest of these is love.
(I Corinthians 13:13)

Eight interrelated triggering events of Paulo Freire's first 20 years of his life left a deep impression on him, which laid the foundation of his life and thought. First, because he "had the possibility to experience hunger" (Horton & Freire, 1990, p. 24), Freire not only learned a great deal about suffering and doing without, but he also captured the meaning of empathy and compassion, and it was then at 11 years old "I vowed to do anything I could do to alleviate hunger in the world" (Freire, 1990a, p. 94).

Second, because he experienced poverty, yet simultaneously had the ability to co-exist with friends within the working class and middle class, he "learned the differences of classes by seeing how their language, their clothing, their whole lives expressed the totality of class separations in society" (Shor & Freire, 1987, p. 28).[1] Third, because of his observation of the hard work, sacrifices, and even abuse his parents were forced to endure, particularly his mother, Freire learned to especially respect those who are in positions of vulnerability and weakness (Freire, 1996).[2]

Fourth, because his parents demonstrated a deep love, which permeated his household, he learned that the security and power of love can play a marked role in coping with life's difficult circumstances. Indeed, Freire learned that the power of love is about lifting up the community (Freire, 1996). Fifth, because of the influence of his parents' spirituality, he learned that faith, if it is to be real, must be one that is demonstrated in concrete action as to how one authentically lives and interacts, particularly with respect to the poor and marginalized (Freire, 1996; Horton & Freire, 1990).

Sixth, despite the painful challenges and hardships that Freire had to endure, he learned not "to accept reality as it was," but in hopeful "critical optimism" as to what it could be (Freire, 1996). Seventh, because he observed and experienced the severe consequence of the greed and exploitation of political, social, and economic systems that further alienated and marginalized the poor, the beginning stages of his radicality began to take shape (Freire, 1996). Finally, the sum total of the triggering events of those early years, which ultimately cemented the foundation of Freire's thinking and greatly empowered his life's work, is succinctly explained in his words with two fundamental beliefs:

1. Because I had experienced poverty, I never allowed myself to fall into fatalism; and
2. Because I had been born into a Christian family, I never accepted our precarious situation as an expression of God's wishes. On the contrary, I began to understand that something really wrong with the world needed to be fixed (Freire, 1996, p. 14).

As Freire moved into adulthood, the evolving development of his faith and the later reading of progressive theologians aided in crystallizing his belief in the necessary social justice role in which the church should involve itself. His work at Serviço Social da Indústria (SESI), his intense involvement with adult literacy campaigns, and his constant reading of a wide range cross–section of educational, philosophical, and political thought radically shaped his politics and the role of education in a democratic society (Kirylo, 2011).

The years he spent in exile, working with the World Council of Churches (WCC) and interacting with diverse individuals from a variety of countries the world over added to the profundity of his thought, particularly regarding his attempt to find unity in diversity, and the building of a more just and ethical world.[3] After his return from exile, he was considerably shaped by monumental personal and work–related endeavors, none more profound than living the agony and the ecstasy of life and death when he entered into his "dark night of the soul" with the passing of his first wife Elza to a rediscovery of the spring of a new life with his marriage to Ana Maria (Nita). Finally, working as Secretary of Education for the municipality of São Paulo and his subsequent ongoing efforts of traveling around the globe giving lectures, consulting for UNESCO, and working on various literacy projects certainly played a tremendous role in the continuous development and refining of his thought and practice (Kirylo, 2011).

With an insatiable desire to learn from the beginning to the end of his life, Freire understood himself as a human being thoughtfully under construction, continuously reinventing his life and work. In that light, he saw life as something that was not predetermined and was intensely aware of his "unfinishedness" and to remain static was not an option; that is, his "epistemological curiosity" was driven by the dialectic of what he knew and what he didn't know and, thus, the desire to be in a continuous, evolving process of learning, growing, and changing (Freire, 2007, 1998).

In the final analysis, the brilliance of Freire's pedagogy of "unfinishedness" was that he possessed the perceptive insight to draw from a diverse range of influences and logically blend them into a unifying educational philosophy, which has led scholars and practitioners from around the world to uniquely identify a way of thinking or teaching that would fall under the singular umbrella of Freirean thought or Freirean action.[4] Schugurensky (1998), remarking on Freire's genius to harmonize his broad range of influences, puts it this way: "Indeed, Freire provided one of the most creative syntheses of twentieth century adult education theory, in which he articulated a language of critique and a language of possibility at a time when it was most needed, particularly in Latin America" (p. 20).

Moreover, Allman et al. (1998) argue that there is an "absolute coherence" in Freire's ability to cite and refer to a wide cross–section of sources in order to articulate his unique thought and practice. In the final analysis, as Elias (1994) asserts, Freire drank from many wells, thus, simultaneously classifying him as "an educational philosopher, a philosopher of knowledge, a social critic, a sociologist of knowledge, an adult educator, a theologian of liberation, and a theorist of revolution...a phenomenologist, an existentialist, a Christian, and a Marxist" (p. 31).

From the beginning of his childhood experiences to the end of his life, Paulo Freire indeed drank from many wells. But the one source, which was firmly planted in his youth which threaded and unified these diverse wells, was grounded in the well of love. In fact, without an unbridled sentimentalism, Freire was that rare academic who was able to extraordinarily convey in such a way that linked love to his critical thought and activism.

To be sure, when the notion of love comes to the forefront of thought or conversation, the concept is inherently shrouded in an air of mystery, which can be difficult to explain, understand, and for some of us, even to realize its power.[5] And while love is naturally a feeling, an emotion, and is the binder that makes the human experience worth living, love can ultimately be characterized as a virtue. This suggests, therefore, that love is more than an emotional response, but rather a state of being regardless of a momentary feeling. In that light, it is thusly worthwhile to first spend a little time exploring the concept of virtue since it is so intimately linked to love. In other words, a conversation on love cannot be devoid of a conversation on virtue.

After an overview of the term virtue and its association to love, the remainder of the chapter will then explore how Freire artfully infused love as the chief cornerstone of his pedagogical work. Indeed, his seminal work *Pedagogy of the Oppressed* (and truly his entire body of work) is a volume that permeates with a flow of love, a love that bends toward justice and equality for all peoples.

AN OVERVIEW OF VIRTUE

When we consider the implications of the word virtue, it is a concept that has arguably sparked more debate, curiosity, and rumination more than any other term in the annals of moral thought (Walter, 1987). We can go as far back to the ancient Greeks, namely to Plato's Republic in which we see virtue as a concept related to moral living and public life, having an influence on western political thinking. And it was Aristotle who not only linked virtue to happiness, but he also suggested that to be virtuous is not something that comes naturally, but it is something that is cultivated through practice and habit. In that light, virtuousness becomes a character state, manifested in the choices one makes in conducting acts of virtue. Aristotle famously coined the phrase *recta ratio agibilium*, meaning "right reason applied to practice" (Walter, 1987; Richert, n.d.).

To that end, originally by definition through the Greeks, the evolution of what is known as the human virtues or more commonly called the cardinal virtues emerge, which are prudence, justice, fortitude, and temperance.[6] The term "cardinal" is significant in that it is a derivative from the Latin *cardo*, meaning "pivot" or "hinge," thus suggesting that these "pivotal" cardinal virtues are what all other virtues hinge on in order to live a moral or virtuous life (Walter, 1987; Richert, n.d.).

While the ancient Hebrews were naturally conscious of the notion of human virtues, there was no term in the Hebrew Scriptures (Old Testament) that intimated a conventional meaning of virtue. However, when the Old Testament was translated from the Hebrew to the Greek (Septuagint), the word *arête* (virtue or excellence) surfaces (see, for example, Wis 4:1 and 5:13). While in the Christian Scriptures (New Testament) the word "virtue" is not often used—perhaps because of the anthropocentric (a central focus on a human driven initiative as opposed to spiritually driven) nature of the word—it was a term that was referred to when it came to moral goodness (see, for example, Philippians 4:8; 1 Peter 2:9; 2 Peter 1:3; 1:5). It is also true, however, that in the early Christian community, especially expressed in the Pauline letters, the notion of virtues was linked to spirituality and not to a human doing, especially when it came to the virtues of faith and love, ultimately the transforming agent of all other virtues (Walter, 1987).

Significantly contributing to a Christian-influenced understanding of virtue came in the 5th century when Augustine of Hippo (Aurelius Augustinus Hipponensis) argued that while from one perspective he saw virtue as an established characteristic of the soul, innately impacting morally right action; but from another perspective he saw virtue as a deliberate act or choice in which one rightly and properly lives. In either perspective, however, Augustine was clear about the link between the Christian life and the place of the cardinal virtues. But it is what is known as the theological virtues (faith, hope, and love) in which Augustine placed supreme importance (Walter, 1987).[7]

As Thomas Aquinas (1981) puts it, the concepts of faith, love and hope are theological virtues because of their eternal significance and because they are "… infused in us by God alone" (p. 851).[8] And above all, it was the theological virtue of love that grounded St. Augustine's thought, famously proclaiming, "Love, and do what you will" (Augustine, n.d.1, para. 8).[9] In other words, Augustine understood that a deep love for God is spiritually transformative, naturally illuminating a whole new way as to how one views self, powerfully impacting a willingness to live a life of faith. What this suggests is that acts of goodness in themselves are not what make those acts virtuous, but it is the love that drives those acts that enables the illumination of virtue. Stated another way, doing "whatever you will" is driven by a profound freedom that has been found in a love relationship with a God who sets one free. As Mother Teresa (1983) so aptly stated, "Love cannot remain by itself—it has no meaning" (p. 75).

THE VIRTUE OF LOVE

Whether one's reflection on the concept of love is framed in a theological context or simply from a "human" point of view (although not always mutually exclusive realities), the concept of love is naturally provoking, shrouded, as earlier mentioned, in a cloud of mystery.[10] And when it comes to distinguishing what love means relative to love for the divine or for another human being or one's love for the poor, truth, justice, or even for country is far different than distinguishing a love for pizza or some other material object (Mcdonagh, 1987).[11]

Fundamental throughout both the Hebrew and Christian Scriptures is God's love for humanity, first manifested through the creation story in which God saw all that was created as good. In this light, God's love is creative, most particularly culminating in the creation of humankind as partners in love with the divine (Mcdonagh, 1987). And yet despite humanity turning itself against its creator, God remained in steadfast love for His people, most profoundly expressed with the sending of His only son to walk and even die among the people. To be sure, the laying down of one's own life for another is the ultimate expression of love.[12]

The depth of God's love, therefore, is one that speaks to the concept of *agape*, a term coming from the Greek, which expresses the highest form of love in which no conditions are placed. In other words, *agape* is the type of love that asks for nothing in return; it personifies love in its greatest conceivable form, realizing by its very nature that it cannot be driven by human effort (Lewis, 1945, p.15). Rather, it is a type of love that is eternal, never ceases, and in theological terms is moved by the action of the Holy Spirit (see I Corinthians 14:1–13). Indeed, it was Martin Luther King, Jr, during the 1960s civil rights struggle, who often talked about how an *agape* form of love must be the cornerstone of the civil rights movement, exhorting all to rise to the level of "God operating in the human heart" (King, 1967, p. 42). In that light, therefore, the life-long journey of realizing the profoundness of an *agape* form of love is one that richly enables us to, as C. S. Lewis (1960) states, "see everything else" (p. ?).[13]

Thusly, the question for human beings is how we respond to God's creative act of creation in seeing everything else, especially in our relationship with God, and in turn how we demonstrate how we treat our neighbor. To the latter, highlighted throughout both the Hebrew and Christian Scriptures, love is demonstrated through action on how we work to set people free from bondage (Exodus story); how we work to further justice (Amos 5); how we work to feed the hungry, take care of the poor, and embrace the stranger (Matthew 25); and, how we work to conduct our lives like the "good Samaritan" (Luke 10).

Indeed, when Jesus introduced himself in a public forum, He announced his mission, declaring, "The Spirit of the Lord is upon me, because he has anointed me to bring glad tidings to the poor. He has sent me to proclaim liberty to captives and recovery of sight to the blind, to let the oppressed go free, and to proclaim a year acceptable to the Lord" (Luke 4: 18–19). In the final analysis, Jesus is the personification of the "God is love" proclamation, and as Mother Teresa pressed, as stated earlier, love by itself has no meaning, suggesting—as it does in 1 John—that it is most profoundly found in relationship and in taking care of the human family.

To that end, love is intimately linked to justice. And doing justice is a social endeavor that engages in the realm of equity, economics, opportunity, education, health care, employment, race, ethnicity, gender and other social and civic constructs. In short, social justice aims to cultivate the common good, working to lift those up who have been historically on the outside looking in, enabling "…them to become active participants in the life of society" (National Conference of Catholic Bishops, 1986, p. 46).

From a historical perspective, the contemporary concept of "social justice" can be traced back to the 1800s by theological and religious circles, and had and still has as its aim to make right the conditions that are unjust, which keep people in poverty or from opportunity. For example, as mentioned in Chapter 8 of this text, see the 1891 encyclical issued by Pope Leo XIII titled *Rerum Novarum* (On the Condition of Workers), which laid the foundation for future social teachings in the Church (Dorr, 1983). Troubled with the horrible living and working conditions of Europe's urban poor, Leo XIII (1942) took a clear position against exploitation in working toward lifting the poor from the miserable living conditions in which they found themselves.

It is worth noting that social justice can be a charged concept, often associated with "leftist" thinking or to progressives to both those in and out of the Church. But the reality is—traced down from the teachings of the Hebrew Scriptures to the Christian Scriptures—the Almighty is a God of justice, culminating with the teachings of Jesus, which suggests "social justice" is not about the right or the left, but rather is something that is inherently shaped in the image of God.

Consider Archbishop Oscar Romero of San Salvador who was and continues to be a powerful voice for the voiceless, taking what Richard Rohr (1987) calls the naked position of the gospel—that is, not placing his affinities to the political left or right. That is, he fervently and persistently proclaimed truth to power intensely calling out structural inequalities or what the liberation theologian would call "institutional sin." In other words, Romero was not about taking a said political position or inflaming politically charged party affiliations as a platform; rather, he was about the seeking of justice and God's ultimate reality of peace and love. Romero (1979) puts it this way,

> It's amusing: This week I received accusations from both extremes–from the extreme right that I am a communist; from the extreme left, that I am joining the right. I am not with the right or with the left. I am trying to be faithful to the word that the Lord bids me preach, to the message that cannot change, which tells both sides the good they do and the injustices they commit. (p. 163)

In the end, therefore, as permeated throughout the Scriptures and exemplified through Oscar Romero's life and work, social justice work must necessarily be informed by love. In other words, "Love *informs* (italicized is author's) all other virtues, lives in them, is their soul force" (Land, 1987, p. 552).

A TRAMP OF THE OBVIOUS WHO LOVED

For Paulo Freire, love indeed was the soul force in which his personal life was bathed, and which illuminated his vision of justice, truth, activism, and his academic work. In fact, Nita Freire (2011), Paulo's widow, emphasizes that Paulo was not only a compassionate man and one who had a great capacity to understand, who possessed a great belief in the goodness of people, but she also makes clear that Paulo's greatest virtue was his consistency, and his ability to love. Worthwhile to quote in its entirety, Nita continues in her characterization of Paulo,

> …But most of all he loved the 'pueblanos,' the working class of Brazil and the world. It was very easy for Paulo to love people, and he taught through the example…He had an incredible presence about him, creating an impact on those around him. Even though he was physically a small man, Paulo possessed the presence of a man of strength. At a gathering or something of that nature, when he walked in a room he somehow commanded a pedagogical presence. With respect to the things he felt, thought, and wrote, it was important to him to maintain a consistency between his private and public life. Paulo was a teacher of himself in the virtues that he wrote in his books. That is, he taught himself consistency, humbleness, tolerance, generosity, compassion, and the ability to authentically listen and love. In other words, Paulo actually lived what he wrote! There was always a great consistency with what he saw, observed, what he reflected, what he wrote, and what he put into practice. The intention of Paulo's work was never for recognition; rather his intention was always to dignify the lives of all men and women. As a way of educating himself, a principal aspect of his philosophy was to continue to ask questions. He always asked himself and stimulated others to ask why? In favor of whom? In favor of what? Against what? Against whom? When Paulo spoke to another individual, he was soft in tone, intently listened, sometimes touching the other person on the shoulder. He had a way of staying in the moment with the individual, giving all of his attention. Paulo had a very simple behavior, never considering himself better or worse than anyone else. (pp. 276–277)

Others who knew Paulo simply affirm Nita's personal and professional observation of Paulo in his capacity to love. For example, among known and unknown people, Shirley Steinberg (2005) characterizes Paulo as one that was imbued with a radical love that blended a spiritual and social commitment as a way of life. Cynthia Brown (2011) saw Freire as a "…lover devoted to the poor and oppressed" (p. 242). For Antonia Darder (2002), she makes clear without question "…that Freire's greatest contribution to the world was his capacity to be a loving human being" (p. 35). Ramón Flecha (2011) declares that along with Pato (Jesús Gómez) and Joe

Kincheloe, "…Paulo Freire is today considered the author of Radical Love, which he practiced throughout his life" (p. 249). Clearly touched by Freire's friendship, Joe Kincheloe (2005) stresses that "His [Paulo's] radical love certainly changed my life and allowed me entrée into a world I was not born to enter" (p. xlvii).

Freire's great capacity to love was rooted in a genuine humility; in that light, however, he also was acutely aware that "loving is not enough; one must know how to love" (Freire, 2005, p. 82). In other words, once again analogous to Mother Teresa's assertion previously mentioned in which she declares love has no meaning if it remains by itself, Freire is, of course, suggesting that love is demonstrated in action, and that this action ought to be informed by love, a love which necessarily leans its arc toward justice. To put another way, as Cornel West (2011) puts it, "Just as justice is what love looks like in public and tenderness is what love feels like in private, deep democratic revolution is what justice looks like in practice" (para 3).

Freire (1985) not only characterized himself as a common man, but he also viewed himself as a "tramp of the obvious" (p. 171). That is, the starting point of his work began with an examination of obvious realities (e.g., illiteracy, joblessness, hunger, etc.). And he found it amusing that his reporting of obvious realities not only attracted attention, but also merited him much criticism, which made apparent to him how the veiling of "the obvious" is a central aspect of hegemony (I. Shor, personal communication, 2010), which is simply the control or influence of one group over another. Consequently, what Freire discovered was that, "the obvious is not always as obvious as it appears" (1985, p. 171).

Perhaps to state another way, Freire's life work focused on examining social phenomena by a deep unearthing of the contradictions that exist within lived realities, which ultimately focused on the dialectical nature between the forces of humanization and dehumanization (Roberts, 2000) (See Chapter 3). Therefore, as Nita Freire underscored above, and to reiterate, a discerning filter that guided Paulo's lens of justice was one that was steered by the following questions: In favor of whom? In favor of what? Against what? Against whom? When it comes to decisions of any kind that interface with various civic, social, structural, and religious affairs, these questions loom large. In other words, do our decisions of any kind lead to the further humanization of our brother, our sister or toward a more dehumanized reality for them?

To be sure, in situations of injustice, in particular, taking a position of neutrality is not an option. Bishop Tutu makes the point that to plead neutrality is to take the side of the oppressor. Tutu cites a simple example: If an elephant were standing on the tail of a mouse, it would have to make a choice of whether to step on the mouse or take a step off its tail. To say there are two sides to the question would not be accurate. For the mouse there is no neutral position. You either take the side of the mouse, or participate in causing its death (Rohr, 1987). This kind of support, or non-support, if you will, was very important to the survival of the system. To that end, Freire's four questions are relevant, and will remain relevant as long as injustice occurs in the world. Our task is to actively, but lovingly, respond to those questions from right where we are when we see inequities in education, health care, and in any other social or civic services that appear to leave some out in fully participating in society.

TEACHING AS AN ACT OF LOVE–DIALOGUE AS DEMONSTRATION OF LOVE

Freire (1984) once said, "I love to be a teacher" (p. 520). This love he speaks about is one that not only suggests a love for others, but also loving the process itself involved in the teaching act which is necessarily laced with joy, seriousness, rigorousness, and preparation (Freire, 2005). Further emphasizing the point, Freire (2005) declares,

> …It is impossible to teach without a forged, invented, and well-thought-out capacity to love…We must dare, in the full sense of the word, to speak of love without fear of being called ridiculous, mawkish, or unscientific, if not antiscientific. We must dare in order to say scientifically, and not as mere blah–blah–blah, that we study, we learn, we teach, we know with our entire body. We do all of these things with feeling, with emotion, with wishes, with fear, with doubts, with passion, and also with critical reasoning. However, we never study, learn, teach, or know with the last only. We must dare so as never to dichotomize cognition and emotion…The teaching task is above all a professional task that requires constant intellectual rigor and the stimulation of epistemological curiosity, of the capacity to love, of creativity, of scientific competence and the rejection of scientific reductionism. The teaching task also requires the capacity to fight for freedom, without which the teaching task becomes meaningless. (pp. 5–6)

A critical cornerstone of Freire's pedagogical approach is to engage in dialogue, and for dialogue to exist, it must rest its foundation in love (Freire, 1990b).

And the beginning point of a dialogical relationship not only assumes that the learner possesses distinct value, but also presupposes that schooling is a dynamic that involves the psychological, cultural, and experiential level of the learner (Freire, 1994). Moreover, the notion of dialogue is not simply a "conversation" as one can find in a contemporary dictionary definition of the term, suggesting that it (dialogue) is merely a sharing of ideas.

Finally, dialogue is more than the Socratic notion of it when Socrates utilizes it as a teaching tool in order for subjects to rediscover forgotten ideas or knowledge (Collins, 1977; Freire, 1985). Rather, for Freire, embedded in the element of dialogue is criticality in problematizing the existential reality of the subject (Freire, 1985).[14] This latter point suggests, therefore, that those who particularly find themselves living in oppressive conditions, the chains of silence must be broken in order to become more fully human. As Freire (1990b) argues:

Human existence cannot be silent, nor can it be nourished by false words, but only by true words, with which men [and women] transform the world. To exist, humanly, is to *name* the world, to change it. Once named, the world in its turn reappears to the namers as a problem and requires of them a new *meaning*. Men [and women] are not built in silence, but in word, in work, in action–reflection…If it is in speaking their word that men [and women], by naming the world, transform it, dialogue imposes itself as the way by which men [and women] achieve significance as men [and women]. Dialogue is thus an existential reality. (pp. 76–77)

Freire's conception of dialogue draws from, among others, the existentialists Karl Jaspers and Martin Buber. Jaspers (1957) argues that being a part of the human family necessitates meaningful relationships, and dialogue is what cultivates the building of those relationships.[15] And for communication to be authentic, it requires "equality, mutual recognition, affirmation, solidarity, questioning, abandonment of ego protection, no quest for victory, unlimited clarification, and no sophistry…" (Jaspers, 1957, p. 89). And Buber (1958) makes the distinction between the *I–it* and the *I–thou* relationship, implying that the former is not only dictated by a monologue type of stance, but also the *I* is the creator of what is and the manipulator of the other, whereas the latter engages the participants in a mutually respectful horizontal connectedness among persons, which is driven by authentic dialogue.

For Freire (1990b) dialogue is indeed an encounter between human beings, and in order for it to be authentic and transformative, the presence of love, humility, hope, faith in humanity, and critical thinking are all necessary aspects to a dialogical relationship. Regarding the necessity of those elements, Freire (1990b) further clarifies the point that *love* suggests courageous action, a commitment to others, and a vehicle to cultivate freedom;[16] *humility* is the recognition of not acting in arrogance and recognizing the other to "name" the world; *hope* is grounded in our incompleteness, which propels the constant search for meaning; *faith in humanity* suggests belief in the power of human beings to stay committed to their ontological vocation to be more fully human; and the engagement of *critical thinking* is what enables dialogue to exist.[17]

CONCLUSION

In the final analysis, Paulo Freire—as an unfinished human being who was desirous of continually growing—was a man who thirsted for justice for all; a man that possessed a disposition that exhibited a sense of prudence, fortitude, and temperance; a man that exuded an obvious humility, living in such a way that illuminated a certain joy and serenity; and, finally, a man who framed his life in a deep faith in God (and humanity), and lived and worked with a sense of hope in humanity. In this light, therefore, Freire was a man of great virtue, which was demonstratively illuminated in the greatest virtue of all as one grounded in the well of love.

NOTES

[1]   Freire explains this co-existence, along with his siblings, as one in which he describes as living as "connective kids," with one foot in a middle class setting and the other experiencing poverty and hunger. To put another way, while Paulo's lack of food was not to the degree of those of many of his classmates, he, nevertheless, still intimately identified with them because he had to somehow deal with his own hunger. In other words, as Freire (1996) puts it, "We participated in the world of those who ate well, even though we had very little to eat ourselves, and in the world of kids from very poor neighborhoods on the outskirts of town. We were linked to the former by our middle–class position; we were connected to the latter by our hunger, even though our hardships were less than theirs" (p. 21). And despite the hardships, even at an early age, Paulo attempted to be positive while at the same time recognizing the contradictory nature of his social surroundings, realizing that something was wrong in the world and it "needed to be corrected" (Freire, 1996, p. 13).

[2]   As a result of the 1929 stock market crash and worldwide economic crises, Paulo's parents' ability to put enough food on the table became extremely challenging. Because at the time the economy of Brazil significantly depended (and still does) on the coffee industry, and because of the market crash, the price of coffee significantly fell, virtually having a negative effect on every aspect of the Brazilian economy. Despite the economic realities, however, Paulo's father continued to work very hard in seeking ways to provide for the family, and his mother attempted the same, only to be rejected in her search for small jobs. Moreover, when she tried to purchase some food on credit, such as with the local butchers, she would have to endure regular harsh rejection and sexist treatment, much to the great, painful dismay of Paulo, who deeply learned from these observations "to respect those who find themselves in a position of weakness or frailty" (Freire, 1996, p. 41).

[3]   Spread out through more than 110 countries and territories, the World Council of Churches (WCC) is comprised of a worldwide community of 349 churches from a diverse group of Christian churches, including scores from the United and Independent churches and those from the Orthodox, Anglican, Baptist, Lutheran, Methodist, and Reformed faith traditions. While the Roman Catholic Church is not an official member of the WCC, many Roman Catholics have always been on staff with the WCC, as was the case with Paulo Freire. With its administrative offices in Geneva, Freire worked as a special consultant to the Office of Education, and in that capacity, through the invitation from such entities as churches, governments, agencies of the United Nations, universities, and social movements, he was invited to examine, consult, and learn about education programs from numerous countries around the world (Freire & Faundez, 1989; http://www.oikoumene.org).

[4]   There were a variety of influences that informed Freire's thought, such as that from the work of Georg Lukács, Louis Althusser, Karl Marx, Frantz Fanon, Mao Tse Tung, Albert Memmi, and Amílcar Cabral, Gilberto Freyre, Francisco Weffort, Fernando de Azeveda, Álvaro Vieira Pinto, Anísio Teixeira, Erich Fromm, Edmund Husserl, Herbert Marcuse, Emmanuel Mounier, Friedrich Engels, Antonio Gramsci, Jean-Paul Sartre, John Dewey, Jean Piaget, Lev Vygotsky, Augustine, and Jacques Maritain, among numerous others, all of which illuminated his understanding of existentialism, phenomenology, personalism, liberalism, Marxism, and his own faith journey which greatly shaped his pedagogical work. For an extensive list of individuals (writers, philosophers, socials scientists, pedagogues, etc.) who impacted Freire's thinking, see A. Freire's notes (note one, tenth letter) of P. Freire's book *Letters to Cristina: Reflections on My Life and Work* (1996).

[5]   Particularly for the latter point, for the nihilist, living in a state of despair or pessimism prevents one from fully realizing the power of love. In other words, as Fromm (1956) argues, nihilism "…is rooted in a destructive attitude toward life, in the willingness to throw away life because one is incapable of loving it. The courage of despair is the opposite of the courage of love…" (pp. 126–127).

[6]   Because he saw prudence linked to the intellect, Thomas Aquinas viewed prudence as the first cardinal virtue, which enables us to make judgments with respect to right and wrong, and the kinds of willful decisions we all make. Particularly in light of seeking wise counsel from others, especially when it comes to complex decisions, seeking prudence allows us to reduce the possibility of making an error. Second to prudence, according to Aquinas, is the cardinal virtue of justice, which emphasizes human rights (Richert, n.d.). Taking its cue from earlier Catholic social teaching (i.e., *Rerum Novarum*

(On the Condition of Workers) (1891), *Quadragesimo Anno* (On the Fortieth Year) (1931)), justice was central to the documents of Vatican II (1962–65), particularly illuminated with the advent of liberation theology (see Chapter 8). Although countless other examples can be made in which known and unknown individuals have linked the Scriptures to social justice, it was Martin Luther King, Jr. who, in his famous 1963 "I have a dream" speech drew from the book of Amos (5:24–27), when he proclaimed in oratorical magnificence that devotees of civil rights will not be satisfied until, "justice rolls down like waters, and righteousness like a mighty stream." Indeed, social justice is about the cultivation of the common good in which all of God's people can equitably, justly, and rightly participate in a civil society. Aquinas contends fortitude (or courage) is the third cardinal virtue, which suggests that despite the various obstacles, fears, or challenges we each face in life, fortitude provides for us the strength to carry on. Particularly with respect to one who defends his/her faith in the midst of persecution, fortitude can also be characterized as a gift of the Holy Spirit. The final cardinal virtue is temperance, which according to Aquinas, is manifested in how we exhibit self-control regarding our carnal desires (e.g., appetite for food, drink, sex, etc.). In other words, temperance provides for us the ability to withhold from excess or abuse (Richert, n.d.).

[7] In addition to the cardinal and theological virtues, there is also what is known as the eschatological virtues (i.e., gratitude, humility, vigilance, serenity, and joy), which in theological terms are given by the Holy Spirit, suggesting there are certain dispositions, values, and times in which these virtues are appropriated in order to live a moral, ethical, and righteous life. Naturally, however, the concept of virtues intersects moral development, having a clear impact on the thinking of Erik Erikson, Jean Piaget, and Lawrence Kohlberg who have significantly contributed to how we grow, develop, process, and learn to deal with the world around us (Walter, 1987).

[8] While the concepts of faith and hope are not the focus of this chapter, it is worthwhile to briefly mention that the idea of faith is naturally associated with one's belief system often expressed in one's religion or spirituality. It is reasonable to assume that the authenticity of one's faith is determined through the manifestation of how one communicates, what is communicated, as well as in behaviors and actions. And while faith is naturally linked to things of the spirit and religious belief systems, there is also the idea of faith expressed in the context of possessing a fundamental faith in the human family, which is revealed in how we relate with one another (for more detail on the concept of faith and its relationship with Freire, see Chapter 1). While hope is a concept that is viewed as a theological virtue, it is also, however, a necessary psychological element that provides for human beings a sense of purpose in order to live meaningfully. As Komonchak, Collins, and Lane (1987) put it, "Hope is the presupposition behind the human 'will to live'" (p. 493). (for more detail on the concept of hope and its relationship with Freire, see Chapter 4).

[9] Augustine (n.d.2) also memorably declared "You have formed us for Yourself, and our hearts are restless till they find rest in You" (para 1). Living a life of excess, attempting to embrace a variety of philosophies of life, and a continuous search for meaning, Augustine eventually came to that place of personal transformation in which his peace and meaning in life rested in his love for the living Christ.

[10] Mystery, as the Franciscan Richard Rohr (2016) describes it, is "...something that you *cannot* understand; rather, it is something that you can *endlessly understand.* There is no point at which you can say, 'I've got it.' Always and forever, mystery gets *you!* In the same way, we don't hold God in our pocket; rather God holds us and knows our internal shape and deepest identity. When we describe God, we can only use similes, analogies, and metaphors. All theological language is an approximation, offered tentatively in holy awe. That's the best human language can achieve. We can say, 'It's like ...' or 'It's similar to ...; but we can never say with absolute certainty, 'It is ...' because we are in the realm of beyond, of transcendence, of mystery. We absolutely must maintain a fundamental humility before the Great Mystery; otherwise, religion worships itself and its formulations instead of God" (para 5–6; italicized is the author's).

[11] Erich Fromm in his classic text, *The Art of Loving* (1956), contends that love is not primarily an entering into a relationship, as it were, but rather love is "...an *attitude,* an *orientation* of *character,* which determines the relatedness of a person to the world as a whole, not toward one 'object' of love" (p. 46, italicized is the author's). In other words, love is a dynamic that emanates from the soul, an activity which reveals itself in various types of love that is uniquely dictated by the object being

loved. Fromm further suggests there are five distinct objects of love. In brief, *brotherly love*, which is foundational to the other four objects of love, is driven by respect, care, and responsibility for the other. As a human family we are all connected as one, implying that as individual human beings we are equals. *Brotherly love* is acutely manifested on how we treat our brother and our sister, especially with respect to those in great need. *Motherly love* is that most unique bond a mother has with her child, the closeness that is established with the sucking of the breast in which "Milk is the symbol of the first aspect of love, that of care and affirmation" (Fromm, 1956, p. 49). While a *motherly love* nurtures the young one with milk, this nurturing also must include a sweetness that raises the child with a proper love that is not overprotective, but rather sprinkled with balance in allowing the growing child to move from dependence to independence, from being completely connected with the mother in the womb, to complete separation as an adult. *Erotic love* is that which desires an exclusive fusion with another person. But this fusion, if it is to be love, is one that originates from the essence of one's being. In this light, as in a committed relationship, *erotic love* is more than a feeling, but also is an act of the will, a decision, a promise. *Self-love* is that which is dictated by self-respect (as opposed to being narcissistic), one that is driven by the implication of the passage, "You shall love your neighbor as yourself" (Mark 12:31). As Fromm (1956) puts it, "The love for my own self is inseparably connected with the love for any other being" (p. 59). Finally, *love of God*, is indicative of the highest good or value. And while a discussion about the love of God is highly complex, this love is freely given and freely received where the divine is both father and mother.

[12] Whether it is Maximilian Kolbe, Joan of Arc, Medgar Evers, Dietrich Bonhoeffer or the numerous first responders that went up the twin towers on 9/11, there are many known and unknown cases in which courageous individuals have given up their lives for the other. And while the ultimate sacrifice of laying down one's life is death, is martyrdom, it is also true that daily—whether one is a person of faith or not—we each have opportunities to lay down our lives in the way we extend a helping hand to a child in need; in the way we take the coat off our back and give it to a brother; in the way we offer a cup of water to a sister; and, in the way we offer our time, talent, abilities, and resources to those in need.

[13] C. S. Lewis (1960), in his notable work, *The Four Loves*, not only clarifies the meaning of *agape*, but he also illuminates three other forms of love (*philia, storge,* and *eros*) as outlined from the Greek. While beyond the scope of this present work to discuss in detail each of these forms of love, in brief, *philia*, expresses a reciprocal type of love, and recognizes our social nature in that "it is not good for man to be alone." As John Donne states, "No man is an island." Moreover, our intrinsic longing to be loved, accepted, and recognized has a natural impact on our emotional and psychological health. Yet, if one is not attuned to its conditional nature, a *philia* type of love can be self-centered and one that simply seeks its own reward. *Storge* relates to a maternal type of love. A mother will naturally love, nurture, and protect her newborn. *Storge* loves simply because it loves; in a sense, it loves because it should. And, while *storge* is not like a *philia* form of love, whereby it is conditional in meeting a certain need or desire, it does, however, have a self-seeking component. For example, as the newborn begins to grow and develop, she begins to discover the notion of discipline. Mom may say to the child, "If you do not clean your room, you will not play outside," or in a more positive tone, "If you clean your room, you will be allowed to play outside." Slowly and progressively, over time, the child begins to discern ways in which her behavior can dictate either positive or negative attention from Mom. In this sense, *storge* may begin to take on a more tenacious conditional tone. To be sure, unless *storge* is fruitfully nourished with "give and take," as Lewis (1960) contends (p. 54), it potentially can evolve into a high level of discord, sometimes leading to estrangement and alienation. Finally, *eros* expresses an esthetic love. In many places in his dialogues, Plato describes this love in the search and longing of the soul for the divine. Today, however, the Greek term *eros* refers to romantic love. Because *eros*, by its very nature, involves the body, mind, emotions, and spirit, it necessitates careful handling; otherwise it can be driven by a self-centered, calculated, and manipulative point of view, leading to what Lewis (1960) describes as finding the "absolute in the flesh" (p. 55). In short, *eros* touches the deepest core of our person, and each of us must be discerning of its profound purpose.

[14] To state in a different way, guiding a dialogical setting possesses a certain purpose and structure that steers the engagement of the object of study (Shor & Freire, 1987; Roberts, 2010). In other words,

for dialogue to be a critical aspect of meaningful learning, it is one then that is an epistemological endeavor whereby the educator maintains her/his epistemological curiosity, while at the same time cultivating her/his critical reflection in a process "of creating pedagogical spaces where students become apprentices in the rigors of exploration" (Freire & Macedo, 1995, p. 384). Dialogue, therefore, fosters a horizontal relationship between educator and learner, which impacts the building of trust whereby the dialogical occurrence begins with the learner as the subject engaged in a process whereby he/she plays an integral role as creator and maker of their world (Freire, 1994). To that end, the notion of dialogue is integral in the process of conscientização (see Chapter 5).

[15] In order to better appreciate the point, it is worth recalling the derivative of dialogue and clarifying the distinct difference between dialogue and monologue. Dialogue is a term that is derived from the Greek, *dia*, which signifies across or through, and *logue*, derived from *logos* (word), meaning speech, conversation or discourse. Also, as the Greek derivative suggests, dialogue implies an exchange between two individuals (or groups/entities), which is obviously different than the notion of a monologue. The latter, with its prefix *mono*, Greek for single or alone, implies that there is no discourse or exchange involved; only one person (or group/entity) speaks. In other words, monologue has no concern for ascertaining a response. Dialogue, however, with its root implication of "coming across" or "getting through," assumes that within the exchange of the word there is another side, another story, another point of view that, respectively, needs to be considered. In short, key to a dialogical relationship is authentic listening (Freire, 1997). The latter, therefore, assumes that the relationship between the educator and the learner is not one of a hierarchal top–down paradigm or one that is of a vertical nature which is played out in an education of domestication manifested through an anti–dialogue stance. Anti–dialogue is not concerned about another point of view; rather its only concern is its own content, its own point of view, its own conquest, and manipulates (Freire, 1990c).

[16] Freire (2005) also characterizes this kind of love as "armed loved," meaning it is a "fighting love of those convinced of the right and the duty to fight, to denounce, and to announce. It is this form of love that is indispensable to the progressive educator and that we must all learn" (p. 74). Darder (2002) describes the latter as a "pedagogy of love" which consists of a political commitment to social justice and the breaking of an exploitive, capitalist system.

[17] In other words, critical thinking "discerns an indivisible solidarity between the world and men [and women] and admits of no dichotomy between them—thinking which perceives reality as process, as transformation, rather than as a static entity—thinking which does not separate itself from action, but constantly immerses itself in temporality without fear of the risks involved" (Freire, 1990b, p. 81).

REFERENCES

Allman, P., Mayo, P., Cavanagh, C., Heng, C. L., & Haddad, S. (1998). Introduction: …the creation of a world in which it will be easier to love. *Convergence, XXXI*(1 and 2), 9–16.

Aquinas, T. (1981). *Summa theologic* (Vol. 2, p. 851, Fathers of the English Dominican Province, Trans.). Allen, TX: Christian Classics: A Division of Thomas More Publishing. (Originally published in English in 1911—copyright 1948 by Benziger Brothers, Inc., NY)

Augustine. (n.d.1). *Homilies on the first epistle of John* (Homily 7) (1 John 4:4–12). Retrieved from http://www.newadvent.org/fathers/170207.htm

Augustine. (n.d.2). He proclaims the greatness of God, whom he desires to seek and invoke, being awakened by Him (Chapter 1). *The Confessions* (Book 1). Retrieved from http://www.newadvent.org/fathers/110101.htm

Brown, C. (2011). In Brown's words. In J. D. Kirylo (Ed.), *Paulo Freire: The man from recife* (pp. 242–244). New York, NY: Peter Lang Publishing.

Buber, M. (1958). *I and thou* (2nd ed.). New York, NY: Scribner.

Collins, D. E. (1977). *Paulo Freire: His life, works and thought*. New York, NY: Paulist Press.

Darder, A. (2002). *Reinventing Paulo Freire: A pedagogy of love*. Boulder, CO: Westview Press.

Dorr, D. (1983). *Option for the poor: A hundred years of Vatican social teaching*. Maryknoll, NY: Orbis Books. (Original work written 1474–1566)

Elias, J. L. (1994). *Paulo Freire: Pedagogue of liberation*. Malabar, FL: Kreiger Publishing Company.

Flecha, R. (2011). In Flecha's words. In J. D. Kirylo (Ed.), *Paulo Freire: The man from recife* (pp. 248–249). New York, NY: Peter Lang Publishing.

Freire, A. (1996). In P. Freire (Ed.), *Letters to Cristina: Reflections on my life and work* (D. Macedo, Q. Macedo, & A. Oliveira, Trans., pp. 191–252). New York, NY: Routledge.

Freire, A. (2011). An interview with Ana Maria (Nita) Araújo Freire (Transcribed and Translated by J. D. Kirylo & A. A. Kirylo). In J. D. Kirylo (Ed.), *Paulo Freire: The man from recife* (pp. 271–289). New York, NY: Peter Lang.

Freire, P. (1984). Conversation with Paulo Freire (W. B. Kennedy, Ed.). *Religious Education, 79*(4), 511–522.

Freire, P. (1985). *The politics of education: Culture, power, and liberation.* New York, NY: Bergin & Garvey.

Freire, P. (1990a). Interview: Paulo Freire. *Omni, 12*(4), 74–94.

Freire, P. (1990b). *Pedagogy of the oppressed.* New York, NY: Continuum.

Freire, P. (1994). *Education for critical consciousness.* New York, NY: Continuum.

Freire, P. (1996). *Letters to Cristina: Reflections on my life and work* (D. Macedo, Q. Macedo, & A. Oliveira, Trans.). New York, NY: Routledge.

Freire, P. (1997). A response. In P. Freire, J. W. Fraser, D. Macedo, T. McKinnon, & W. T. Stokes (Eds.), *Mentoring the mentor: A critical dialogue with Paulo Freire* (pp. 303–329). New York, NY: Peter Lang.

Freire, P. (1998). *Pedagogy of freedom: Ethics, democracy, and civic courage.* Lanham, MD: Rowman and Littlefield Publishers, Inc.

Freire, P. (2005). *Teachers as cultural workers: Letters to those who dare teach* (Expanded Edition). Boulder, CO: Westview Press.

Freire, P. (2007). *Daring to dream: Toward a pedagogy of the unfinished* (Organized and presented by Ana Maria Araújo Freire, A. K. Oliveira, Trans.). Boulder, CO: Paradigm Publishers.

Freire, P., & Faundez, A. (1989). *Learning to question: A pedagogy of liberation.* New York, NY: Continuum.

Freire, P., & Macedo, D. P. (1995, Fall). A dialogue: Culture, language, and race. *Harvard Educational Review, 65*(3), 377–402.

Fromm, E. (1956). *The art of loving.* New York, NY: Harper & Row Publishers.

Horton, M., & Freire, P. (1990). *We make the road by walking: Conversations on education and social change* (B. Bell, J. Gaventa, & J. Peters, Eds.). Philadelphia, PA: Temple University Press.

Jaspers, K. (1957). *Reason and existing* (W. Earle, Trans.). New York, NY: The Noonday Press.

Kincheloe, J. L. (2005). Introduction. In P. Freire (Ed.), *Teachers as cultural workers: Letters to those who dare teach* (expanded edition, pp. xli–xlix). Boulder, CO: Westview Press.

King, Jr., M. L. (1967). *Where do we go from here: Chaos or community?* New York, NY: Harper & Row Publishers.

Kirylo, J. D. (2011). *Paulo Freire: The man from Recife.* New York, NY: Peter Lang.

Komonchak, J. A., Collins, M., & Lane, D. A. (1987). (Eds.). *The new dictionary of theology.* Collegeville, MN: The Liturgical Press (A Michael Glazier Book).

Land, P. (1987). Justice. In J. A. Komonchak, M. Collins, & D. A. Lane (Eds.), *The new dictionary of theology* (pp. 548–553). Collegeville, MN: The Liturgical Press.

Leo XIII. (1942). *On the condition of the working classes (Rerum Novarum).* Boston, MA: St. Paul Books & Media.

Lewis, C. S. (1945). *Is theology poetry.* Oxford Socratic Club: Samizdat Press. Retrieved from http://augustinecollective.org/wp-content/uploads/2016/06/1.2-Is-Theology-Poetry-Reading.pdf

Lewis, C. S. (1960). *The four loves.* San Diego, CA: A Harvest Book, Harcourt Brace and Company.

Mcdonagh, E. (1987). Love. In J. A. Komonchak, M. Collins, & D. A. Lane (Eds.), *The new dictionary of theology* (pp. 602–616). Collegeville, MN: The Liturgical Press.

Mother Teresa. (1983). *Words to love by....* Notre Dame, IN: Ave Maria Press.

National Conference of Catholic Bishops. (1986). *Economic justice for all: Pastoral letter on Catholic social teaching and the U.S. economy.* Washington, DC: United States Catholic Conference.

Niebuhr, R. (1927). *Does civilization need religion?* New York, NY: The Macmillan Company.

Purpel, D. (1989). *The moral and spiritual crisis in education: A curriculum for justice and compassion in education*. New York, NY: Bergin & Garvey.

Richert, S. P. (n.d.). *The cardinal virtues*. Retrieved from http://catholicism.about.com/od/beliefsteachings/tp/Cardinal_Virtues.htm

Roberts, P. (2000). *Education, literacy, and humanization: Exploring the work of Paulo Freire*. Westport, CT: Bergin & Garvey.

Roberts, P. (2010). *Paulo Freire in the 21st century*. Boulder, CO: Paradigm Publishers.

Rohr, R. (2016, September 12). *Trinity: MIA* (Week 1). Retrieved from https://cac.org/trinity-mia-2016-09-12/

Rohr, R., O. F. M. (1987). *Beyond our cultural biases: Siding with the cosmic Christ*. Cincinnati, OH: St. Anthony Messenger Tapes.

Romero, O. (1979/1988). In J. Brockman, S.J. (Ed.), *The violence of love: The pastoral wisdom of Archbishop Oscar Romero* (Translated and compiled by J. R. Brockman, S.J.). New York, NY: Harper & Row.

Schugurensky, D. (1998). The legacy of Paulo Freire: A critical review of his contributions. *Convergence, XXXI*(1&2), 17–28.

Shor, I., & Freire, P. (1987). *A pedagogy for liberation: Dialogues on transforming education*. New York, NY: Bergin & Garvey.

Steinberg, S. (2005). Afterword. In P. Freire (Ed.), *Teachers as cultural workers: Letters to those who dare teach* (expanded edition, pp. 173–178). Boulder, CO: Westview Press.

Walter, J. J. (1987). Virtue. In J. A. Komonchak, M. Collins, & D. A. Lane (Eds.), *The new dictionary of theology* (pp. 1081–1085). Collegeville, MN: The Liturgical Press.

West, C. (2011, November 18). A love supreme. *The Occupied Wall Street Journal*. Retrieved from http://occupiedmedia.us/2011/11/a-love-supreme/

A MAN WHO HUMBLY LIVED
IN AUTHENTICITY

To be authentic it must be liberating. One of its basic preoccupations must be the greater penetration of the 'prise de conscience' which operates in human beings when they act and when they work.

(Freire, 1994, p. 148)

Those who authentically commit themselves to the people must re–examine themselves constantly.

(Freire, 1990, p. 47)

People who met Freire or heard him speak often identified the quality of humility as one of his distinguishing character traits.

(Roberts, 2000, p. 16)

Conscientização (conscientization) (see Chapter 7) is not a process that is static, nor formulaic; rather it is a process that assumes an understanding of our unfinishedness and the critical place of the dialectical interweaving of reflection and action (praxis), implying that this understanding is a "requirement" in becoming more authentically human "if we are to deepen our awareness of our world, of facts, of events, of the demands of human consciousness to develop our capacity for epistemological curiosity" (Freire, 1998, p. 55). In that light, therefore, when we consider the concept of authenticity and its relationship to becoming more authentically (or fully) human, it not only intersects with Freire's conception—that as unfinished beings—to fully live is to be in a continuous process of reinventing oneself, but also suggests that one (as subject) is true, honest, and genuine to oneself, and—therefore—to others.

The question then becomes what do we mean by the term "authenticity" and, further, how is it associated with the virtue of humility? Moreover, as Peter Roberts' epigraph indicates, Freire was a man of humility, clearly as evidenced to those who knew him. How was it then that such a well-known, accomplished academic able to rest his foundational character in the virtue of humility, particularly within the world of the academy where it is not uncommon to observe academic types who remain high on their own self-importance? To that end, this chapter aims to explore those two fundamental questions in light of Freire's spirituality.

THE PRAXIS TOWARD LIVING AUTHENTICALLY

To authentically live suggests that the conscious self acts true according to one's self–understanding and ethical "code" that s/he has freely constructed in order to provide meaning and purpose in life. Indeed, if one is not true or ethical to his/her created meaning and purpose, then life is naturally lived inauthentically, ultimately leading to anxiety, despair, and meaningless living (Heidegger, 1996).[1]

Thus, the autonomous nature of the concept of authenticity is liberating in the sense that one acts out of commitment and choice as opposed to a sense of duty. In other words, instead of filtering one's interpretation and meaning of the world through institutional or other external constructs, a person of authenticity explores meaning through existential experiences (Maslow, 1968; Heidegger, 1996), not only revealing a transparency of his/her humanity, but also paving a path to becoming a subject of his/her history (Collins, 1977).

However, because oppression is a vehicle to domesticate, the consequence for the oppressed is the thwarting of the ability to become subjects of history naturally impacting the capability to be authentically human. Stated another way, to live authentically is to possess the opportunity to authentically live, implying that instead of history "given" and "received," history is grasped and made, which begins with a critical examination of reality. In other words, as Collins (1977) puts it, "Men [and women] exist authentically when they can name the world, giving meaning to history and culture, they can only name it when they know it authentically" (pp. 65–66).

As highlighted in Chapter 3, dehumanizing infrastructures subvert choice and freedom for the oppressed and oppressor, and both are in need of liberation in order to be more authentically human. For the former, a ridding of themselves of being "hosts" of the oppressor, which is maintained by their unawareness of the conditions that have propelled them to "fatalistically 'accept' their exploitation," all of which gives them an "unauthentic view of the world and of themselves" (Freire, 1990, p. 51).

And for the latter, "Any situation in which some men [and women] prevent others from engaging in the process of inquiry is one of violence…to alienate men [and women] from their own decision–making is to change them into objects…No one can be authentically human while he [or she] prevents others from being so" (Freire, 1990, p. 73). Movement toward authentic living, therefore, demands a profound rebirth, a conversion to the people, a critical viewing of reality (see Chapter 2), which richly takes place through dialogue (see Chapter 5) (Freire, 1990), all of which "…is joined by meaningful praxis" (hooks, 1994, p. 47).

The word *praxis* comes from the Greek, meaning to act or do, and the "doing" was associated with political activity. Thus, one who is engaged in political matters is a person of action, marked by the term praxis; and one who lives a life of contemplation (theory) is immersed in the things metaphysical and eternal truths, which stands taller than praxis, yet both are critical aspects of being human. Indeed, the theory–practice tension finds its roots in Greek philosophy (Gutiérrez, 1990).[2]

Immanuel Kant—who placed great importance on the practical and experience yet saw its connection to theory—had an influence on the dialectical thinking of Hegel and others, ultimately leading to Marx, who saw the notion of praxis as central to societal transformation. While Hegel (2010) argued that reality could be understood through a dialectical triadic system of thesis, antithesis, and synthesis, culminating in the metaphysics of the Absolute Idea or Spirit, Marx, albeit holding onto Hegel's concept of alienation and a dialectical perspective of history, rejected his idealism and instead asserted a philosophical perspective that was materialistic, particularly manifested in the "dialectic between economic conditions and human action, or what has been called 'the materialist conception of history'" (Ozmon & Craver, 1990, p. 313).

Thus, drawing on Hegel's transformation of consciousness and the transformation of nature as asserted by Marx, Freire developed his own concept of praxis which is illuminated in his conception of conscientization (Schubeck, 1993). Moreover, borrowing from Gramsci's notion of Marxism as a "philosophy of praxis" and history as one of becoming, and pulling from Kosik's belief that finding our authentic selves occurs through an examination of our daily existential realities, Freire (1985) and Freire and Faundez (1989) argue that humans are incomplete and their move toward becoming and shaping history unfolds through praxis. In other words, through the process of conscientization, the notion of praxis can be characterized as the dialectical interweaving of reflection and action, ultimately playing a significant role in human liberation and societal transformation.[3]

The engagement of praxis obviously implies an ongoing dialectical process, which significantly aids in diminishing "the distance between what we say and what we do" (Freire, 1993, p. 22). Moreover, the dichotomizing of practice and theory contradicts the notion of praxis; that is, theory devoid of practice amounts to simple verbalism; and practice devoid of theory results in blind activism (Freire, 1985). As Freire (1985) puts it, "That is why there is no authentic praxis outside the dialectical unity, action–reflection, practice–theory. In the same way, there is no *theoretical context* if it is not in a dialectical unity with the *concrete context*" (p. 156).

WITH RESPECT TO THE EDUCATOR

For the educator in particular, therefore, fostering a dialogical environment that is filtered through the dialectical interweaving of reflection and action is one that cultivates what Freire (1990) characterizes as a problem-posing approach to the teaching and learning process. In this approach, the driving assumptions are that people are viewed as conscious beings who are unfinished, but yet are in the process of becoming; liberation occurs through cognitive acts as opposed to the transfer of information; the vertical structure of teacher–of–the–students and students–of–the–teacher as in banking education is not visible,[4] but rather a horizontal relationship that materializes through a teacher–student with students–teachers; that is, a joint responsibility between student and teacher exists and a non–dichotomizing interaction is evident, implying both are actively engaged as co–investigators in the pedagogical process (Freire, 1990).

Particularly in light of Freire's concept of cultural circles[5] as the frame of practice, a problem–posing approach unfolds in a dialogical setting that explores and problematizes existential realities. In other words, the process is one where students are presented with problems relative to themselves and their relationship with the world, leading them to be challenged yet prompted to respond to that challenge within a context of other interrelated problems.

Because of the concreteness of the problems posed as opposed to the exploration of theoretical questions, the resulting outcome is one of critical comprehension and less alienation, leading to new challenges, new understandings, and commitment to the process. In short, problem–posing education is one where human beings "develop their power to perceive critically *the way they exist* in the world *with which* and *in which* they find themselves; they come to see the world not as a static reality, but as reality in process, in transformation" (italicized is author's) (Freire, 1990, pp. 70–71).

And while love is what laces a dialogical environment in which a problem-posing approach to education is propelled, it is humility which must ground the educator in order to come to that greater sense of fostering an authentic faith in humankind (Freire, 1971). As Rohr (2013) puts it, "…love works only inside humility" (p. 166).

HUMILITY

In the higher and admirable sense of the word, humility describes one as modest, unassuming, and unpretentious. From a spiritual perspective, the characteristic of humility genuinely places ego to the side, allowing one to authentically yield and to be open to God (or the transcendent), others, and to grow in wisdom. In other words, as Nouwen (1983) asserts, "It [humility] means staying close to the ground (*humus*), to people, to everyday life, to what is happening with all its down–to–earthness. It is the virtue that opens our eyes for the presence of God on the earth…" (p. 162).

Thus, humility necessitates a letting go of preconceived notions of what is, who we are, and perhaps even who God is. Mother Teresa (1996) suggests that the reality of truth cannot be spoken without simultaneously considering the value and necessity of humility. In that light, Freire (2005) makes the point, "Humility helps us to understand this obvious truth: No one knows it all; no one is ignorant of everything. We all know something; we are all ignorant of something…Humility helps me avoid being entrenched in the circuit of my own truth" (p. 72). Hence, in the act of teaching, one is also in the primal position to learn from students, implying a profound respect for them and taking the time to listen to them.

While humility, as described above, is demonstrated through modest behavior, keeping one close to the ground, and guides the certainty–uncertainty tension of our truth, it does not imply a resignation, cowardice, or disrespect for oneself; in fact, "humility requires courage, self–confidence, self–respect, and respect for others" (Freire, 2005, p. 72). Stated another way, humility can be characterized as the ability to admit limitations and weaknesses, leading to a clearer understanding of oneself; the ability to thoughtfully discern biases and prejudices, leading to tolerance, acceptance, understanding, and empathy; the ability to recognize and determine that one's lens of the world may quite possibly be too narrow and limiting, leading to a more holistic perspective; the ability to admit that one may not be as informed as he/ she ought, leading to a pursuit of knowledge and information; the ability to discern a healthy ego as opposed to being egotistical; the ability to get in touch with and constructively address what Carl Jung calls our shadow—that is, those areas in our lives that, in large part, are associated with negativity, insecurity, and discomfort; and the ability to accept individual strength, insight, knowledge, wisdom, and intelligence as gifts that are to be nurtured, refined, and ultimately used as a service to others.

In short, the virtue of humility, which informs our incompleteness, is a critical component of a progressive teacher, one who embraces the process of becoming, while at the same time realizing that no one is above or superior to anyone else (Horton & Freire, 1990; Freire, 1995; Freire, 1998). In the end, humility, combined with love, powerfully aids one to embrace the virtue of tolerance, which "teaches us to learn from and respect the different" (Freire, 2005, p. 76).

AN INCREDIBLE PRESENCE

Ana Maria (Nita) Araújo Freire (2011) describes Freire's spirituality as one that was authentic, making clear he was a man who carried "an incredible presence about him," further stating that "…it was important to him to maintain a consistency between his private and public life," which was not only grounded in his aim to live a life of "…consistency, humbleness, tolerance, generosity, and compassion," but also in his ability to authentically listen (p. 276).[6] In other words, Freire was one who lived what he wrote, with a deep love for people, especially a love for "…the 'pueblanos', the working class of Brazil and the world" (p. 277).

As Nouwen earlier reminds us, to live in humility is to stay close to the ground, to the real, to people, something that Paulo Freire intimately understood, which is the reason why Cone (2011) can easily say that Freire's life "embodied" humility.[7] And Cone further points out that "Humility will always keep you knowing that it is not just about you" (p. 206). And therein lies the salient point.

To live in humility is to realize its power, its presence. And to realize its power and presence is to live authentically. And to realize the dynamic of authenticity is to realize the dialectical interweaving of reflection and practice. And to realize this entire process is to realize that to engage in the world is to engage with the other, and that life is not *just* about you. This is something that Freire deeply understood in his spirit, in his being.

Indeed, Paulo Freire was that rare academic who filtered his life in the act of becoming by living what he wrote. For more than some that walk the halls of the academy, many get caught up in "their" research; "their" work; "their" expertise; "their" status, etc. And what often gets lost in that process is that ultimately their work is not about them, especially for those of us in education, social work, or any other social justice work. It is always about the other, as Freire so understood.

NOTES

[1] Heidegger, who emphasized the notion of what is characterized as existential phenomenology, focused on the concept of "acting in history" and "being in the world" or in Heideggerian terms *Dasein* (existence), the way one interacts and subjectively negotiates life's experiences (Kluback & Wilde, 1958).

[2] According to Pythagoras, metaphysical contemplation is characterized as *theoria* (theory), and the philosopher who lived the "theoretical" life was close to the gods, and thus living happily. Influenced by the thinking of Pythagoras, Aristotle's conception of *theoria* implied that contemplation was an endeavor reserved for philosophers who engaged in the divine activity of contemplating things universal and timeless (Schubeck, 1993).

[3] Collins (1977) explains it the following way:

> Liberation comes about through conscientization when men [and women] "take possession" of reality by demythologizing it and acting upon it. As praxis it is an unfinished process because discovering a new reality by critical transitivity does not exhaust conscientization. The new reality must become the object of a new reflection since what is authentic in one historical epoch will not necessarily be authentic in another...The more men [and women] are conscientized the more they exist. Freire compares the entire process of conscientization to a "painful birth" or an "Easter experience" in which human consciousness of the oppressor and the oppressed dies in order to be reborn. (p. 65)

[4] A banking education is driven by the following assumptions: first, it views people as those who are manageable and adaptable; second, the teacher sees reality as compartmentalized and one that is static and predictable; third, students learn through memorization as per what knowledge is dictated by the teacher; and fourth, a dichotomy exists between a person and the world. That is, one is *in* the world as spectator as opposed to *with* the world as re–creator (Freire, 1990). To that end, banking education is driven by the thinking that students, from a Lockean *tabula rasa* (blank slate) perspective, are empty receptacles, or what Freire (1970) refers to as "empty pots" in need of filling by the teacher, who is the possessor of knowledge. In other words, this kind of educational approach is regulated and one of depositing whereby "the students are the depositories and the teacher is the depositor" (Freire, 1990, p. 58). This kind of educational approach thwarts creativity, reinforces a fatalistic outlook, and functions through a monologue or anti–dialogical stance. And because the cultural–socio–historical setting is not contextualized, the existential reality of the learner is not a consideration simply because "knowledge is a gift bestowed by those who consider themselves knowledgeable upon those whom they consider to know nothing" (Freire, 1990, p. 58). In the final analysis, a banking education is one that Freire (1990) describes as necrophilic (see Chapter 3, endnote 13), an approach that is extraordinarily controlling, all in an effort to obviate thinking, maintain the status quo, and serve the interest of the oppressor.

[5] It was through the adult education programs that were conducted by Freire that the notion of cultural circles and cultural centers had its beginnings, forming at such venues as soccer clubs, neighborhood associations, churches, and philanthropic organizations. Frame–worked in an approach that utilized pictures or slides to introduce topics, while at the same time encouraging dialogue with the participants, various themes such as nationalism, democracy, development, and illiteracy were discussed in these circles. The success of that process prompted Freire and his associates to think about how the notion

of cultural circles could be used to actually teach adult learners how to read (Freire, 1996). That is, because of the obvious interest of the participants in the adult education programs, Freire theorized that a major aspect for adult literacy learners to learn how to read must begin with the process of them reading their concrete *world*, which naturally would lead to a greater critical consciousness of their reality, ultimately facilitating an energy and enthusiasm to learning to read the *word* (Brown, 1978).

[6] It is worth pointing out that the term compassion, which is intricately linked to the qualities of empathy and care, comes from the Latin *compati*, meaning to be conscious and aware of another's difficulty and distress while simultaneously seeking out possible solutions and alternatives to alleviate anxiety and troubles. Therefore, as it relates to the concept of care, Mayeroff (1971) makes the point that the idea of caring is not an abstract concept, or a momentary event, but rather a way of relating to with another. In other words, the process of caring aids in facilitating growth, relationship, and especially illuminates itself in realizing another's potential, possibilities, particularly when facing obstacles and times of difficulty.

[7] There was a mutual respect between Paulo Freire and James Cone, who is known as the "father" of a black theology of liberation. Freire wrote the Foreword to Cone's 1986 edition of *A Black Theology of Liberation*, which also appears in Chapter 11 of Freire's text *The Politics of Education*. Speaking of Cone, Freire (1985) writes "James Cone is a committed man, 'saturated' in this real world, which he analyzes with the authority of one who has experienced it" (p. 148).

REFERENCES

Brown, C. (1978). *Literacy in 30 hours: Paulo Freire's process in north east Brazil*. Chicago, IL: Alternative Schools Network.

Collins, D. E., S. J. (1977). *Paulo Freire: His life, works and thought*. New York, NY: Paulist Press.

Cone, J. (2011). Paulo Freire, Black theology of liberation, and liberation theology: A conversation with James H. Cone. In J. Kirylo (Ed.), *Paulo Freire: The man from recife* (pp. 195–212). New York, NY: Peter Lang.

Freire, A. (2011). An interview with Ana Maria (Nita) Araújo Freire. In J. Kirylo (Ed.), *Paulo Freire: The man from recife* (pp. 271–289). New York, NY: Peter Lang.

Freire, P. (1970). *Cultural action: A dialectic analysis* (Cuaderno No. 1004. APDO. 479). Cuernavaca, Mexico: Centro Intercultural de Documentacion (CIDOC).

Freire, P. (1971). To the coordinator of a "cultural circle." *Convergence, 4*(1), 61–62.

Freire, P. (1978). *Pedagogy in process: The letters to Guinea–Bissau*. New York, NY: The Seabury Press.

Freire, P. (1985). *The politics of education: Culture, power, and liberation*. New York, NY: Bergin & Garvey.

Freire, P. (1990). *Pedagogy of the oppressed*. New York, NY: Continuum.

Freire, P. (1993). *Pedagogy of the city*. New York, NY: Continuum.

Freire, P. (1994). *Education for critical consciousness*. New York, NY: Continuum.

Freire, P. (1995). The progressive teacher. In M. de Figueiredo–Cowen & D. Gastaldo (Eds.), *Paulo Freire at the institute* (pp. 17–26). London, England: The 'Brazilian Educators' Lecture Series Institute of Education, University of London.

Freire, P. (1996). *Letters to Cristina: Reflections on my life and work* (D. Macedo, Q. Macedo, & A. Oliveira, Trans.). New York, NY: Routledge.

Freire, P. (1998). *Pedagogy of freedom: Ethics, democracy, and civic courage*. Lanham, MD: Rowman and Littlefield Publishers, Inc.

Freire, P. (2005). *Teachers as cultural workers: Letters to those who dare teach* (expanded edition). Boulder, CO: Westview Press.

Freire, P., & Faundez, A. (1989). *Learning to question: A pedagogy of liberation*. New York, NY: Continuum.

Gutiérrez, G. (1990). *The truth shall make you free* (M. O'Connell, Trans.). New York, NY: Orbis Books.

Hegel, G. W. F. (2010). *The philosophy of history* (J. Sibree, Trans.). New York, NY: Digireads.com Publishing.

Heidegger, M. (1996). *Being and time*. Albany, NY: State University of New York Press.

hooks, b. (1994). *Teaching to transgress: Education as the practice of freedom*. New York, NY: Routledge.

Horton, M., & Freire, P. (1990). *We make the road by walking: Conversations on education and social change* (B. Bell, J. Gaventa, & J. Peters, Eds.). Philadelphia, PA: Temple University Press.

Kluback, W., & Wilde, J. T. (1958). Power and freedom. In M. Heidegger (Eds.), *The question of being* (W. Kluback & J. T. Wilde, Trans., pp. 27–31). New York, NY: College and University Press Services.

Maslow, A. (1968). *Toward a psychology of being* (2nd ed.). Princeton, NJ: Van Nostrand.

Mayeroff, M. (1971). *On caring*. New York, NY: Harper & Row, Publishers.

Mother Teresa. (1996). *Mother Teresa: In my own words* (Compiled by J.–L. G. Baldo). New York, NY: Gramercy Books.

Nouwen, H. J. M. (1983). *Gracias: A Latin American journal*. New York, NY: Orbis Books.

Ozman, H., & Craver, S. (1990). *Philosophical foundations of education* (4th ed.). Columbus, OH: Merrill Publishing Company.

Roberts, P. (2000). *Education, literacy, and humanization: Exploring the work of Paulo Freire*. Westport, CT: Bergin & Garvey.

Rohr, R. (2013). *Immortal diamond: The search for our true self*. San Francisco, CA: Jossey-Bass.

Schubeck, T. L., S.J. (1993). *Liberation ethics: Sources, models, and norms*. Minneapolis, MN: Fortress Press.

CHAPTER 7

CONSCIENTIZATION

Inner and Outer Transformation for Liberation

BLACK LIVES MATTER

On April 11, 2012 George Zimmerman, a member of an Orlando community's town watch program, was charged with the second-degree murder of Trayvon Martin, a 17-year-old black male returning from a corner store where he had purchased a drink and some candy. A struggle ensued and Zimmerman shot and killed Martin. While Zimmerman claimed he was acting in self-defense, the Florida State Attorney claimed that Martin was not a threat and charged Zimmerman on that basis. After lengthy pre-trial deliberations and extensive media coverage, jury selection for the trial began in May 2013 and the trial began on July 11. After sixteen hours of deliberation over the course of two days, the six-person jury rendered a verdict of not guilty on all the charges against Zimmerman.

When news of the verdict became public, Alicia Garza, a community organizer from Oakland, California wrote a *Facebook* post entitled "A Love Note to Black People." In the posting she wrote "Our Lives Matter. Black Lives Matter." Patrisse Cullors, a friend and fellow community organizer in Los Angeles, read the posting and created the hashtag #BlackLivesMatter. Opal Tometi, a sister organizer based in Phoenix, Arizona, had experience with social media and helped spread the hashtag on the Internet. With this simple online interaction between three black women, the Black Lives Matter (BLM) movement was born. Like so many other African Americans, the three women had reached a point where a protest against the pattern of violence against black people needed to be initiated.

One year later in August 2014, BLM came into wider public view when they organized a Black Lives Matter Freedom Ride to Ferguson, Missouri, to call attention to the shooting death of Michael Brown by police officer Darrin Wilson. After a St. Louis grand jury investigation, Wilson was not indicted for the shooting. Demonstrations emerged in the Ferguson area and all over the country. While BLM was only one of many groups involved in the demonstrations, it eventually emerged as the most visible. Later that year on the day after Thanksgiving, so called "Black Friday," fourteen BLM activists led by Alicia Garza were arrested in San Francisco for delaying the public train for more than an hour. In December over 2000 people gathered at the Mall of America in Bloomington, Minnesota to protest the killings of unarmed black men; there the slogan "Black Lives Matter" was used.

Since 2014, BLM has spread to communities across the United States and Canada. The slogan "Black Lives Matter" has become a slogan and call to action against unjustifiable killings of black people at the hands of police. While drawing on the Civil Rights Movement slogan "None of us are free until all of us are free," BLM has widened the sphere of oppression to include members of the LGBT and Womanist communities. BLM has been quite adept at using social media to mobilize its members quickly for marches, die-ins and other disruptive actions in response to local and national events (Ruffin, n.d.; Day, 2016; Anonymous, n.d.). Then in July 2015, BLM held a national gathering in Cleveland attended by 1500 activists where there were strategy sessions and a chance to evaluate the status of the movement going forward. BLM uses a decentralized leadership model (leader-full). While some BLM chapters continue peaceful marches and demonstrations, others have been more confrontational, calling for economic boycotts, and more public accountability for officers involved in shootings (Eligon & Smith, 2015).

On their website and in their literature, BLM explains its focus this way: "When we say Black Lives Matter, we are broadening the conversation around state violence to include all the ways in which Black people are left intentionally powerless at the hands of the state. We are talking about the ways Black lives are deprived of our basic human rights and dignity" (Anonymous, n.d.). The statement goes on to list issues such as disproportionate poverty among People of Color, mass incarceration, the treatment of undocumented immigrants, the neglect of people with disabilities, and discrimination of members of the LGBT community. The statement concludes: "#Black Lives Matter is working for a world where Black lives are no longer systematically and intentionally targeted for demise" (Anonymous, n.d.).

Though it has been twenty years since his death, and over 50 years since he was expelled from his native country of Brazil, Paulo Freire would recognize in the Black Lives Matter movement the pattern of socio-political and cultural awareness leading to action to challenge and change the world; he called this process conscientization. While essentially a pedagogical and political concept, conscientization carries within it an implicit spirituality that guided and encouraged Freire's thought his career.

THE NATURE OF CONSCIENTIZATION

Conscientization or the Portuguese word "Conscientização" is so central to Freire's pedagogical and political philosophy that we can give only an abridged overview here. While conscientization reflects the heart of Freire's theory of teaching and learning (Elias, 1976), he lays no claim to originating the term. He first encountered the word at a 1964 meeting of professors at the Brazilian Institute of Higher Studies. At that gathering Freire understood conscientizacao to represent the idea that education is an act of freedom inviting the learner to take a critical approach to understanding reality. While the word in English is most closely associated with Freire, he claimed it was Father Dom Hélder Câmara, the Roman Catholic bishop of Recife, who popularized it first (Freire, 1974b). By the early 1980s Freire had ceased using the term because it was too often confused with mere consciousness. Nonetheless, the term with all it distortions continues to be used and attributed largely to him (Kennedy, 1984).

For Freire conscientization is more than just awareness or consciousness, but rather a critical apprehension of reality that moves one to action. Through conscientization, the person moves beyond being a passive recipient of whatever life dishes out, to becoming an active participant with other oppressed persons in shaping and changing their world. Conscientization enables a group of people to transcend the limits of their own experience and become aware of the social, political and cultural forces and to see how those forces and the structures they create impact people's lives. For the oppressed conscientization implies that the oppressed can liberate themselves and transform their oppressive conditions. As the oppressed become more aware of the complexity of their situation, they are forced to ask whether and how they will choose to act. At times the historical and political situation may not allow for effective action, but by definition one does not practice conscientization without the possibility of acting against their oppression (Freire, 1974b).

By his own account Freire refined his understanding of conscientization during the 15 years in Brazil and Chile when he was primarily teaching peasants who were illiterate how to read. Freire describes in detail the process he used in teaching *campesinos* to read in *Education for Critical Consciousness* and the third chapter of *Pedagogy of the Oppressed*. Prior to the teaching process, Freire and his associates would spend time with the people going through their daily lives, working in the fields, fixing meals, and so on. The purpose of this pre-teaching work was to become intimately aware of the people's context. Then artists who were part of Freire's team would create pictures of the people's daily lives called "codifications." The participants would then be drawn into a culture circle and the formal teaching would begin, although the people had already unknowingly been teaching Freire and his team.

Referring to the codifications, the teacher would choose an item to begin teaching how to read. Portuguese and Spanish (the primary languages of Brazil and Chile) tend to be phonetic languages where understanding single sounds helps the learner build a wide variety of words. However, at the same time Freire instructed his teachers to engage learners in dialogue about the nature of the world in which they lived. As Freire writes "Reading the world always precedes reading the word…For this reason, I have always insisted that words used in organizing a literacy program come from what I call the 'word universe' of people who are learning…Words should be laden with the meaning of people's existential experience, and not the teacher's experience" (Freire & Macedo, 1987, p. 35). In Brazil the very act of teaching campesinos to read was part of a larger political program to enable the learners to pass a literacy test required of all voters. In this way the Socialist government under which Freire worked sought to secure its political standing against the ruling oligarchy in Brazil. However, beyond the overt political reason, Freire endeavored to engage the peasants in a critical examination of their socio-political reality, and thereby take actions to challenge the cultural, economic, and political forces that kept them poor and marginalized.

The underlying assumption in the conscientization process is that the people have been conditioned to accept their poverty and oppression as their destiny or fate. So they do not question or challenge the restrictions placed on them educationally, economically, socially or culturally. In Freire's terms they have been conditioned to accept themselves as *objects* of the larger society that dehumanizes and oppresses them. By contrast conscientization assumes that all persons, regardless of their social or economic station in life are *subjects*, actors who are free to shape and direct their own lives (Freire, 1993). However, in order to empower people who regard themselves as objects rather than subjects, the first task is to encourage them to engage in reflective action, challenging the unchallenged myths of their existence. Freire writes: "But since, as we have seen, [people's] consciousness is conditioned by reality, conscientization is first of all the effort to enlighten [them] about the obstacles preventing them from a clear perception of reality. In this role, conscientization effects the ejection of cultural myths that confuse the people's awareness and makes them ambiguous beings" (Freire, 2000, p. 64). In other words, the people need to be helped to see that negative and limiting capacities attributed to them need to be examined and debunked.

STAGES OF CONSCIENTIZATION

However, this process of making them aware of the false and destructive beliefs and myths circumscribing their lives is a long and complicated process. Reflecting on the history of Brazilian society in the first half of the 20th century, Freire identifies three general stages of the conscientization process. The first stage is what he calls *semi-intransitivity of consciousness*. At this stage people are living on the edge of survival and so the totality of their existence is wrapped up in meeting their basic biological needs. Their challenges or problems are attributed either to their own failings as human beings or the fate of their existence. They have no awareness that their impoverished status may be due to forces beyond their conscious experience. The challenge for the teacher at this point is to engage the person in dialogue with questions designed to have them look at forces outside their personal realm, to see that the reason for the disenfranchisement may be due to socio-political factors they have not considered.

As people move from blind acceptance of their lot to questioning it, they move from intransitivity to transitivity. They now are beginning to see beyond themselves. Freire says this shift makes a person "permeable," and the person may become actively engaged to understand the larger forces limiting and oppressing him/her. This leads to the second stage which Freire calls *naïve transitivity*. While the person is beginning to mentally transcend her immediate situation, there is a tendency to oversimplify the problem and look for quick and unrealistic situations. While one is more aware at this stage of conscientization, there is also a tendency to shy away from the complexity of issues and the need for deeper and more critical analysis. People tend to think in polarities and look for magical, simple solutions.

If not before, at this point in the process, the person or group of learners is encouraged in researching and addressing the problems they see, and to begin the learning by action and reflection referred to as praxis. As people learn, either through research or trial and error, their understanding of the challenges and problems becomes more sophisticated and complex. If they persist, they will eventually enter the stage of *critically transitive consciousness.* According to Freire, this stage "is characterized by depth in the interpretation of problems; by the substitution of causal principles for magical explanations; by testing one's 'findings' and by openness to revision; by the attempt to avoid distortion when perceiving problems and to avoid preconceived notions when analyzing them; by soundness of argumentation; by the practice of dialogue rather than polemics..." (Freire, 1974, p. 14).

Now at times, individuals and groups will divert from *critically transitive consciousness* and instead adopt what Freire called a *fantasized consciousness*, a stage where people back away and disengage from the reality, and choose to respond emotionally rather than rationally. At this stage groups often become vulnerable to powerful and charismatic leaders who stir their emotions to act in ways that are contrary to their group and personal self-interest. They can become quite fixed in their views and are not open to dialogue. While they have a perspective that includes the social, political and cultural dynamics, they back away from engaging the issues in all their complexity and instead seek simplistic or untenable solutions. For instance, they may turn to religion for some divine intervention, or idealism, where simply thinking about the problem is all that is needed to solve it.

Ultimately, the goal of conscientization is that people come to a place where they can both denounce the structures that are oppressing them, and announce a new vision of the kind of situation or society they desire. He writes, "Conscientization clearly has to do with utopia. The more we are conscientized, the more we become, by the commitment that we assume to change things, announcers and denouncers" (Freire, 1972a, p. 6) (see Chapter 4). This ability to both denounce and announce leads people to become actively engaged in shaping their history, and to develop hope that their situation can and will be transformed (Freire, 1974, 2000; Schipani, 1988).

PRAXIS AND COMMUNITY

As mentioned above, what distinguishes conscientization from consciousness or awareness is the commitment to actively engage the issues identified through social, cultural and political action, and to then reflect on how the action went to refine or improve upon it. This action-reflection dynamic is referred to as praxis. Praxis is what distinguishes conscientization from mere awareness or consciousness.

Freire's emphasis on praxis is a move away from the dichotomy that often exists between theory and action; for him praxis is theory-in-action in an ongoing process of action-reflection and refinement of one's theory of change. The origin of the term is attributed to Aristotle, then refined by Hegel and Marx. Freire drew his understanding largely from Marx with his emphasis on the call of human beings to influence and shape their history. However, from Hegel he drew on the principle of Geist, a force in history moving it toward actualization. It is through and because of praxis that conscientization leads to knowledge and a clearer grasp of one's reality (Freire, 1973; Johns, 1993).

Furthermore, this praxis is not done by isolated individuals, but in community. Freire (2000) writes: "Only praxis in the context of communion makes conscientization a viable project. Conscientization is a joint project in that it takes place in a [person] among other [persons], united by their action and by their reflection upon that action and upon the world" (pp. 58–59). This led Freire to institute the use of culture circles in which the teacher would engage the learners in dialogue and debate. Thus, whether discussing basic literacy skills, or issues of national import such as democracy or the causes of poverty, learners did so in dialogue with each other, and moved through the levels of conscientization and into action as a group.

Schipani (1988) summarizes Freire's understanding of conscientization as "a process of cultural action in which women and men are awakening to their sociocultural reality, move beyond the constraints and alienations to which they are subjected, and affirm themselves as conscious subjects and co-creators of their historical futures" (p. 13). Schipani continues: "It is at the level of praxis that conscientization occurs in the Freirean sense because conscientization implies 'a critical insertion into history', i.e. a willful personal involvement or historical commitment in order to remake the world. And critical awareness leads not only to analysis and understanding, but also to the means for transformation together with others who assume the roles as subjects" (pp. 13–14). Conscientization is a disciplined process that leads a group from awareness to action designed to shape their situation and challenge oppressive structures constraining them. Rejecting their position as passive objects in history, the oppressed act as subjects shaping history through the process of conscientization (Schipani, 1988).

THE IMPLICIT SPIRITUALITY OF CONSCIENTIZATION

As discussed in Chapter 8, Freire's interaction with and influence on liberation theology has been and continues to be significant. In regard to his view of conscientization, the emphasis on praxis, the development of base communities as religious adaption of the culture circle, the use of dialogue to raise people's awareness of unjust structures, and a commitment to address that injustice can be attributed to Freire's influence on liberation theology (Gutiérrez, 1973; Schipani, 1984, 1988). Still others have found conscientization instructive in an understanding of conversion (Self, 1992; Welton, 1993), discipleship (Johns, 1993), spiritual formation and creativity (Schipani, 1984, 1988). Elias (1976) goes so far as to consider Freire a "radical religious reformer." However, how did Freire himself relate his spiritual views and practice to the process of conscientization? In this regard, Schipani (1988) says Freire had an "implicit theological foundation or infrastructure of his pedagogy" (p. 30), and borrowing from Schipani, we want to suggest that in regard to his views on conscientization, Freire also had an implicit spirituality. In other words, Freire does not link his description of conscientization explicitly to an interaction with God, but we get hints from his writings what his underlying assumptions are.

Freire (1972b) relates his faith to the process of conscientization, and it is clear that for him his spirituality was expressed most clearly living out his beliefs and conviction. He wrote "I imagine one of the prime purposes that we Christians ought to have … is to get rid of any illusory dream of trying to change man [sic] without touching the world he lives in…. As a matter of fact, it is idle to talk of changing man without changing also the concrete circumstances he lives in" (p. 11). The purpose of conscientization is so people will "cease seeing reality ingenuously, but to begin seeing in a fresh and more realistic dialectic." Reflecting on his own exile from Brazil, he warns of the ruling elites by whom they "will be damned as enemies of the Christian Western civilization." Speaking personally, he says, "In the final analysis the Word of God is inviting me to recreate the world, not for my brothers' domination, but for their liberation. I am not able to hear that Word, then, unless I am fired up to live it fully" (1972b, p. 12). In this letter it is clear that Freire's commitment to conscientization as a means to people's liberation was ultimately an outward expression of his inward commitment (Freire, 1972). In these words Freire echoes the words of the New Testament' Letter to James: "As the body without spirit is dead, so faith without deeds is dead" (James 2.26 NIV).

In another letter to a seminarian, Freire (1984) echoes a similar sentiment. He writes,

> I cannot know the Gospels if I take them simply as words that rest in me, or if, seeing myself as empty, I try to fill myself with these words… On the contrary, I understand the Gospels, well or badly, to the degree that, well or badly, I live them. I experience them and in them experience myself through my own social practice, in history, with other human beings. (p. 548)

The process of conscientization that Freire taught is modeled in how he sought to know and practice the Biblical truths he believed to be true. The truth was not in the knowing, but in the doing. He concludes that letter by saying: "To know the Gospels through seeking to practice them, within the limits imposed by my finitude, is, thus, the best way I have of teaching them" (p. 548).

Freire also believed that the Latin American context in which he worked and developed his pedagogical philosophy held a special role in shaping the theological thinking of his day. Having been raised in a time when the Roman Catholic Church underwent radical changes both in Latin America and throughout the world with Vatican II, he saw himself participating in a transformative historical moment. He wrote: "I am not a theologian, but merely an onlooker intrigued by theology, which has indelibly marked what my pedagogy seems to be developing into. Still I get the impression that the Third World, by its utopian and prophetic nature as an emerging world could be the inspirational source of this theological renaissance" (Freire, 1972c, p. 14). He then goes on to call Christians to join in solidarity with the oppressed in the task of liberation (Freire, 1972c). There is a clear sense that Freire saw himself living in a critical epoch in history, an epoch in which he felt called to become fully engaged.

While it is clear that Freire saw his work and the process of conscientization to be an outward expression of his Christian faith, he did not see the work of liberation as God's work, as it were, but as the work of the people. Freire (1996) stated this distinction clearly when he wrote: "The person who has reached conscientization and is a believer sees God as a presence in history, but not one that makes history in lieu of men's and women's actions. In fact, it is up to us to make history and to be made and remade by it" (p. 183). God provides the vision, but it is up to the people to bring that vision of the future into reality (For a more detailed discussion of Utopia, see Chapter 4).

Underlying Freire's belief in conscientization was a deep faith in the capacity of humanity to fulfill its potential for freedom (Schipani, 1988). Freire (1996) held to "a certain understanding or view of human beings as managing their nature in their own history, of which they become necessarily both subject and object... I cannot understand human beings as simply living... I can understand them only as beings who are makers of their 'way', in the making of which they lay themselves open to or commit themselves to the "way' that they make and therefore remakes them as well" (p. 97). Coupled with his faith in humanity was his love for humanity, particularly the oppressed who because of their oppression have their inherent human dignity hidden from them. The process of conscientization is also a process of humanization, that is of becoming more human, more fully the persons they were created and destined to be.

Speaking specifically of his view of human beings in the process of conscientization, he says "man [sic] is a being who exists *in* and *with* the world" (Freire, 2000, p. 39). As such, human beings have the ability to stop and observe the world, analyze, and then act on that analysis. They have the capacity to transcend their existence, see beyond their limitations and take action to change the world that limits them. He was clear that conscientization was not some "magical" process but rather possible because of human beings' capacity to know and change their reality. Even as he acknowledged the oppressors and their entrenched self-interest in keeping people in their place, he maintained a firm faith in the people's ability to move toward their liberation, and liberate their oppressors in the process (Freire, 2000).

However, as important conscientization is to the liberation process, it is not a comfortable or painless process. He relates conscientization to childbirth and the Easter experience:

> Bringing together all the things I have said, we see that conscientization is a
> painful birth. There is no palliative for it like those exercises women use to

avoid birth pangs. Conscientization also involves an excruciating moment, a tremendously upsetting one, in anyone who begins to conscientize himself [sic], the moment when he [sic] starts to be reborn. Because conscientization demands an Easter. That is, it demands that we die to be born again. (1972a, p. 10)

To go through the process of conscientization requires both an inner and outer transformation, a conversion of sorts to the oppressed and to the process of liberation (For a fuller discussion of the Easter experience, see Chapter 2).

While Freire has been criticized by those who would wish him to have a more mainstream Christian theological view, it is clear that the essence of Freire's spirituality is rooted in a dialectic between a God present and involved in history, and human beings who are called to be the primary actors in and on that history. In order to join the liberating process conscientization requires a significant inner and outer transformation. Freire saw himself as integrally involved in that dialectic, seeking to empower oppressed persons objectified and dehumanized by oppressive structures to see, analyze and act to bring about greater justice in the world.

CONCLUSION

As one considers the emergence of the Black Lives Matter Movement, the parallels between now and Freire's early days in Brazil are hard to miss. He was part of a literacy movement that challenged and eventually ran afoul of the ruling elite—in the same way BLM has brought awareness on the injustices suffered by people of color at the hands of government officials, particularly police. Through the use of social media, they have created cyber-spaces and physical spaces for oppressed persons to dialogue about their situations and the forces causing them. They have been moved to action, and then have reflected and continued to learn. This commitment to praxis and learning as one goes helps the movement stay nimble and flexible. They have both denounced the injustices inflicted on people of color and they have announced a clear vision: "a world where Black lives are no longer systematically and intentionally targeted for demise" (Anonymous, n.d.). Freire stopped using the word conscientization because of misunderstanding and misuse, particularly in Western contexts. Yet, in later writings he picked up the theme once again, further reinventing its meaning, assuring that the spirit which he brought to conscientization and which shaped his application of it continues to live on. It continues to challenge us toward a future only we can create.

REFERENCES

Anonymous. (n.d.). About the Black lives matter network. *Black Lives Matter*. Retrieved from http://blacklivesmatter.com/about/

Day, E. (2015). *#BlackLivesMatter: The birth of a new civil rights movement*. Retrieved from https://www.theguardian.com/world/2015/jul/19/blacklivesmatter-birth-civil-rights-movement

Elias, J. (1976). *Conscientization and deschooling: Freire's and Illichs' proposals for reshaping society*. Philadelphia, PA: Westminster Press.

Eligon, J., & Smith, M. (2015, August 15). After protests for racial justice, activists ask: What next? *New York Times*. Retrieved from http://www.nytimes.com/2015/08/16/us/afterprotestsforracialjustice activistsaskwhatnext.html?nlid=44534153&src=recpb&_r=0

Freire, P. (1972a). Conscientizing as a way of liberating. *LADOC Keyhole Series*, 3–10

Freire, P. (1972b). A letter to a theology student. *LADOC Keyhole Series*, 11–12.

Freire, P. (1972c). The third world and theology. *LADOC Keyhole Series*, 13–14.

Freire, P. (1974). *Education for critical consciousness*. New York, NY: Continuum.

Freire, P. (1974b). Conscientisation. *Cross Currents*, 23–31.

Freire, P. (1984). Know, practice and teach the gospels. *Religious Education, 79*, 547–548.

Freire, P. (1993). *Pedagogy of the oppressed, 30th anniversary edition* (M. B. Ramos, Trans.). New York, NY: Continuum.

Freire, P. (1996). *Letters to Cristina: Reflections on my life and work* (D. Macedo, Q. Macedo, & A. Oliveira, Trans.). New York, NY: Routledge.

Freire, P. (2000). *Cultural action for freedom* (Harvard Educational Review Monographs). Cambridge, MA: Harvard University.

Freire, P., & Macedo, D. (1987). *Literacy: Reading the word & reading the world*. New York, NY: Bergin & Garvey.

Gutiérrez, G. (1973). *A theology of liberation: History, politics and salvation* (Sr. C. Inda & J. Eagleson, Trans.). Maryknoll, NY: Orbis Books.

Johns, C. B. (1993). *Pentecostal formation: A pedagogy among the oppressed*. Sheffield, England: Sheffield Press.

Kennedy, W. (1984). Conversation with Paulo Freire. *Religious Education, 74*(1), 511–522.

Ruffin, H. (n.d.). Black Lives Matter: The growth of a new social justice movement. *BlackPast.org*. Retrieved from http://www.blackpast.org/perspectives/black-lives-matter-growth-new-social-justice-movement

Schipani, D. (1984). *Conscientization and creativity: Paulo Freire and Christian education*. Lanham, MD: University Press of America.

Schipani, D. (1988a). *Religious education encounters liberation theology*. Birmingham, AL: Religious Education Press.

Schipani, D. (1988b). Conscientization, liberation and creativity. In D. Schipani (Ed.), *Religious education encounter liberation theology* (pp. 9–67). Birmingham, AL: Religious Education Press.

Self, C. (1992). Conscientization, conversion and convergence: Reflections on base communities and emerging Pentecostalism in Latin America. *The Journal of the Society of Pentecostal Studies, 14*(1), 59–72.

Welton, M. (1993). Seeing the light: Christian conversion and conscientization. In P. Jarvis & N. Walters (Eds.), *Adult education and theological interpretations* (pp. 105–123). Malabar, FL: Krieger Publishing Co.

A FREIREAN IMPRINT ON
LIBERATION THEOLOGY

Paulo Freire is considered one of the founders of liberation theology. He was a Christian that lived his faith in a liberating way…Paulo placed the poor and oppressed at the center of his method, which is important in the concept of preferential option for the poor, a trademark of liberation theology.

(Boff, 2011, p. 241)

With plumes of white smoke spiraling out of the small chimney atop the famous Sistine Chapel in the early evening of March 13, 2013, the electricity of excitement was radiating off the thousands of onlookers who were gathered at St. Peter's Square. The white smoke signaled the 266th pope had been elected. Cardinal Jorge Mario Bergoglio of Argentina, the first pope from the Americas, would take the name Francis. Assuming that name was more than a mere symbolic gesture for the new pontiff, like the same spirit of deep faith, simplicity, humility, and a profound love for the poor that guided Francis of Assisi over 800 years ago, Pope Francis has been one that has exuded those same charismas throughout his ministry as a Jesuit cleric in Buenos Aires.[1]

The thrust of Pope Francis' ministry is one that seeks a poor Church that possesses a heart for the poor, which is clearly making its mark on his pontificate. This desire of Francis is not only rooted in the Gospel message, but it is also the same message that is filtered through Catholic social teaching. It is, therefore, no great coincidence that only a few months after he shouldered the papacy, Pope Francis invited Father Gustavo Gutiérrez to Rome, holding private conversations and concelebrating Mass (Cox, 2013).

A brilliant theologian from Peru, the now eighty-five-year-old Gutiérrez is often referred to as the "father"[2] of liberation theology, a theological perspective that centrally places the concept of "preferential option for the poor" as its analytical starting point. Liberation theology, however, has historically been a "thorn in the flesh" for the institutional Church, and while it has not outright rejected its theology, the Church has always been more than slightly uncomfortable with theologians drawing from Marx as a critical lens to examine injustice.

In other words to state differently, because of Gutiérrez's theological thought, he has generally been viewed with suspicion from the hierarchy, even with leanings to censure him.[3] In short, therefore, the significance of Gutiérrez's meeting with the Pope was more than perfunctory and was no small thing;[4] rather, the invitation was an affirming signal to the universal church that a theology of liberation was fundamentally rooted in the Gospel message. Indeed, in the 266th Pontiff, Gutiérrez sees a Church with a "change in atmosphere" (San Martín, 2015, para. 2).[5]

That change of atmosphere indeed caught the attention of Ana Maria (Nita) Araújo Freire. The widow of Paulo Freire, Nita requested a visit with Pope Francis, and he graciously obliged, receiving her at the Vatican in April, 2015. Discussing Freire's work, which Francis has read, Nita not only sees Freire's writings as "more relevant today than 20 years ago," but also saw in Pope Francis one who is creating "a new face of the church" that has the plight of the poor in the forefront of his ministry (Ieraci, 2015).

And while Paulo Freire was a Catholic, and believed in Jesus Christ, he was not one who was caught up in religiosity or the institutional church, as it were; he was, however, a man who richly contributed to the thinking of liberation theology, as underscored by Boff in the epigraph (Ieraci, 2015; Kirylo, 2011). The question, therefore, is what is liberation theology and how did Paulo Freire contribute to the fostering of its thought and action? To that end, the rest of this chapter will explore how liberation theology emerged on the scene, will examine critical aspects of its thinking and action, and will weave in how Paulo Freire impacted the shaping of liberation theology.[6]

CONTEMPORARY HISTORICAL CONTEXT

The "modern" emergence of liberation theology began in 1891 when Pope Leo XIII issued a Catholic social doctrine called *Rerum Novarum* (On the Condition of Workers); it was this encyclical that laid the foundation for future social teachings in the Catholic Church (Dorr, 1983).[7] Pope Leo XIII was troubled with the horrible living and working conditions of Europe's urban poor. He took a clear position against exploitation in trying to resolve the misery of the poor "…since the great majority of them live undeservedly in miserable and wretched conditions" (1942, p. 6). Forty years later in 1931, observing the fortieth anniversary of *Rerum Novarum,* Pope Pius XI released *Quadragesimo Anno* (On the Fortieth Year), which spoke out against economic exploitation and argued the shortcomings of liberal capitalism.

While Leo XIII focused on structural reform, he also concentrated on personal sin and thus called for internal reform. However, Pius XI also viewed sin in a collective sense, asserting that injustice and economic exploitation were committed because of the shortcomings of liberal capitalism (Smith, 1991). After Pope Pius XI, Pope Pius XII also contributed to the social teachings of the Church, and though he espoused the right of private ownership, he "…insisted that this limited right must be subordinate to the interests of the common welfare and the broad right of all people to benefit from the wealth of the earth" (Smith, 1991, p. 85). These Catholic social teachings by Popes Leo XII, Pius XI, and Pius XII through the 1950s functioned as the preparation for the social teachings of Pope John XXIII and Pope Paul VI.

The combined papal teachings of all these popes were later used as the grounding of the modern emergence of liberation theology in justifying their social analytical positions (Smith, 1991).

In 1961, Pope John XXIII issued *Mater et Magistra* (Christianity and Social Progress), which instructed against any new means of colonialism and exploitation in the form of economic, cultural, and/or political rule. John XXIII argued that property owners should act responsibly and even be compelled by law to do so (Gremillion, 1976). In his 1963 encyclical, *Pacem in Terris* (Peace on Earth), he officially pronounced that the Church was committed to the action of democracy, human rights, and religious freedom (Sigmund, 1988). On October 11, 1962, Pope John XXIII made the opening address of the Second Vatican Council. This council "… rather unexpectedly developed into one of the most significant events in the whole history of the Roman Catholic Church" (Hennelly, 1990, p. 39).

It (the council) shifted the Church from a conservative and authoritarian stance to one that supported democracy, human rights, social justice, and political pluralism. Moreover, the Church encouraged a more open line of communication with bishops, clergy, laity, and other Christian denominations and religions (O'Brien & Shannon, 1977). Vatican II's *Pastoral Constitution of the Church in the Modern World* (Gaudium et Spes, 1965) fervently cried out against technological, economic, and political oppression. A postcouncil encyclical *Populorum Progressio* (On the Development of Peoples) focused on world development concerns, with particular attention on lifting the quality of life of those who daily confront hunger, poor living conditions, sickness, poor health care, and no opportunity for formal education (Pope Paul VI, 1967).

SYNODS OF LATIN AMERICAN BISHOPS

Gustavo Gutiérrez gave a presentation for the first time which he called *A Theology of Liberation* at a 1968 conference sponsored by a group of Catholic priests in Chimbote, Peru. A few months later of that same year in Colombia, the Medellín Bishops' Conference was held, which was influenced by the presence of Gutiérrez and other progressive clergy. Titled *The Church in the Present–Day Transformation of Latin America in the Light of the Council*, the purpose of the conference was called to put into action in Latin America the proposals that came out of the Second Vatican Council.

Rooted in the Exodus story of the Hebrew Scriptures and Jesus' first public announcement of bringing "good news to the poor and setting the captives free" (Luke 4), the term "liberation" clearly emerged from Medellín, particularly as a response to unjust economic, agricultural, industrial, cultural, and political realities which clearly violated basic human rights (Los Textos de Medellín, 1977). In addition, based on a Freirean model of "liberating education," the concept of "participation" was illuminated as a result of the conference (Lernoux, 1980). Without question, Medellín, thus significantly impacted Latin American politics; in essence, it dismantled the traditional alliance of the military, the oligarchy, and the Church (Lernoux, 1980).

In 1969, at a Commission on Society, Development and Peace (SODEPAX) meeting, which was jointly sponsored by the World Council of Churches and the Pontifical Commission on Justice and Peace in Cartigny, Switzerland, Gutiérrez gave a presentation similar to the one he gave in Peru the year before (as stated above). Titled *Notes on a Theology of Liberation*, Gutiérrez presented the fundamental framework of liberation theology, ultimately leading to the 1971 publication of his decisive work *A Theology of Liberation*.

The book is a theological reflection on the social, political, and economic conditions of the poor in Latin America and was powerfully influential, prompting Dorrien (1990) to state, "Gustavo Gutiérrez is the most influential figure in modern liberation theology, and arguably the most significant theologian of the past generation. No one has made a greater impact on the shape or direction of theological discussion in our time" (p. 101). After *A Theology of Liberation* was written, many works in liberation theology were promptly published which exerted a powerful influence on the revision of traditional theology and the way liberation of the poor was viewed.[8]

Whereas Medellín significantly challenged the social, political, religious, and political establishment, and whereas the Latin American Bishops' Conference of 1979 in Puebla reaffirmed the proposals of Medellín, it was the Puebla conference which most famously introduced the concept of "preferential option for the poor," which was later reaffirmed at the 1992 Latin American bishops' conference in Santo Domingo, and still later in 2007 at the Fifth General Conference of the Bishops of Latin America and the Caribbean in Aparecida, Brazil (Gutiérrez, 2015, 2013a; Brown, 1990).

IMPACT OF THE PROTESTANT CHURCH

The movement within the Roman Catholic Church during the 1960s was evident in addressing human rights violations and economic injustice. However, simultaneously among Protestants, a church and society movement was formed that was called *Iglesia y Sociedad en America Latina* (Church and Society in Latin America) (ISAL). Sponsored by the World Council of Churches (WCC), Richard Shaull, a Presbyterian missionary to Brazil and one who wrote the Foreword to Freire's English translation of *Pedagogy of the Oppressed*, led the ISAL movement (Smith, 1991). Through ISAL, Shaull and other Protestant theologians were developing what was called a "theology of revolution," which chiefly explored whether revolution had theological implications (Berryman, 1987), all of which was influential in the development of liberation theology (Smith, 1991).[9]

The intention of a theology of revolution did not imply a violent insurgency, but, through the efforts of churches, a Christian justification to take an assertive role in moving toward radical social structure transformation (Smith, 1991). Moreover, resonating in a tone redolent of the German theologian Dietrich Bonhoeffer,[10]

Rubem Alves, a Brazilian Presbyterian theologian involved with ISAL, argued that God is found among the weak, poor, and marginalized. Alves (1969) sought for a theological language whereby a fostering of freedom and justice must be cultivated in order to part from the atmosphere and climate of oppression.

Jose Miguez Bonino, an Argentinean theologian and Methodist minister, not only served as president of the World Council of Churches (WCC), but was also influential in the development of liberation theology in Latin America, arguing that theology must unfold from the lens of the poor and oppressed in their encounter with the Bible (Schubeck, 1993; Ferm, 1986). Moreover, for Bonino (1975), being in solidarity with the poor implies not only obedience to the God of love and justice, but also argues for institutional and structural reform.

THE FORMATION OF ECCLESIAL BASE COMMUNITIES

As a result of the thinking of progressives in the Catholic and Protestant churches, theologians were making both personal and theological links to constructively challenge the societal, political, and hierarchical status quo in Latin America (Smith, 1991). Consequently, *campesinos*[11] and clergy alike organized a network of *comunidades eclesiales de base* (ecclesial base communities), which spread out in many areas of Central and South America.

In the *comunidades eclesiales de base*, the participants prayed, reflected upon and discussed the Scriptures, the documents of Vatican II, Medellín, and Puebla in terms of their struggle for justice and freedom from political oppression.[12] In fact, it was because of Vatican II and the subsequent Latin American Bishops' Conferences that impacted not only the unfolding of a theology of liberation, but also compelled many clergy to work in solidarity with the poor. Moreover, particularly with respect to the documents of the Medellín conference, a Freirean influence was apparent with his conception of conscientization, further radicalizing a contingent of clergy to work with the poor in order to guide the process for them to understand their reality and actively participate in forming a new society (Berryman, 1987).

TAKING A POSITION OF NON-NEUTRALITY

In other words, a position of non–neutrality was visibly taken, affirming Freire's (1985) contention that the Church cannot view itself as neutral; in essence, as long as it does not act in opposition to the oppressors, by default, it is acting on the oppressors' behalf. Thus, a church that critically analyzes inequitable social structures, denouncing oppression and announcing institutional change and radical transformation, and concretely acts on behalf of those who have been historically marginalized, is one, as discussed in Chapter 4, that Freire (1985) characterizes as the prophetic church, as opposed to the traditionalist church or the modernizing church.

In the end, the various church documents described earlier in their proclamation of moving word to action is authentically manifested in the prophetic church, one that accepts its becoming, is not neutral, and does not hide its preference (Freire, 1985). The notion of non–neutrality was extraordinarily disturbing for the establishment. That is, in the 1960s and prior, the Church was rarely subjected to persecution and, in fact, was respected, enjoying a privileged position and harmonious relationships with governments. However, particularly during the time of the Medellín Conference and the attention given to the plight of the poor, governments saw a growing threat of this non-neutrality stance from clergy and certainly others, ultimately getting the attention of the 1969 Rockefeller Commission hearings which argued that if the Catholic Church acted on the thinking of Medellín, the Church could be dangerous in obstructing stability in the region (Planas, 1986).

Moreover, later in 1980, under the Reagan Administration, the Committee of Santa Fe advocated for the U.S. government to take the offense in impeding the progress of liberation theology and those in the Catholic Church in Latin America who were proponents of it. The Santa Fe document even went so far to encourage turning a blind eye toward brutal Latin American dictators who worked hard to snuff out liberation theologians and others in the progressive movement (Müller, 2015).

Yet, despite the U.S. led assault on liberation theology, the dam was broken in the heartened effort by a variety of progressive, prophetic voices to dismantle the establishment. Among those critical voices, in addition to Freire and others, there was also the powerful presence of his friend, Dom Hélder Cámara, auxiliary Bishop of Rio de Janeiro and later Archbishop of Recife and Olinda, who criticized inequities of the economic system.[13]

Cámara was a deeply spiritual person who was universally recognized as an authentic man of God and one who was an ardent defender of the poor. Characterized as "the red bishop," Cámara was unwavering in the assertion that he was not a subversive, a Marxist, or a communist, simply declaring the establishment's contradiction and manipulation, "I feed the poor, I'm called a saint. I ask why the poor have no food, I'm called a communist" (Lalli, 1999, p. 1). A man who clearly inspired, Cámara was greatly involved in the formation of the National Conference of Brazilian Bishops in 1952 and the Latin American Episcopal Conference (CELAM) in 1955. Additionally, he was instrumental in the 1961–1967 Basic Education Movement (MEB), which was based on Freire's problem–posing approach to literacy (Smith, 1991).

Another representative example of pushing back on the establishment was in Colombia, where a radical priest, Camilo Torres, organized a "United Front" to bring together peasants, slum dwellers, workers, and professionals to work for social change in 1965. The steadfast consistency between his words and actions prompted great admiration from many people, thrusting Torres into a kind of iconic state, as if he instinctively anticipated the becoming of a new way of being in the form of what was to be later known as liberation theology (Berryman, 1987).

Though many in the clergy were radically motivated to change inequities, Torres was one of very few priests who joined the guerrilla movement. He lived among the campesinos, rejected any priestly privileges, worked with adult literacy learners, and only ate what little food was available. Torres, like Che Guevara, became a guerrilla, because they were lovers of humanity and felt that the perpetuation of injustice, exploitation, and oppression was dehumanizing action and contradicted all notions of love (Freire, 1985).[14]

Freire was not one to condone violence, nor to participate in utilizing arms in his struggle for a more liberated humanity. As a matter of fact, Freire, as in the case of Torres and Guevara, viewed their revolutionary praxis as one that simply fought against the oppressive conditions that subjected masses of people into an existence of silence. Thus, for Torres and Guevara, the picking up of arms was not one of perpetrating violence, but a legitimate reaction of self–defense and, indeed, an act of love (Roberts, 2000).[15] As Freire (1990c) asserts, "Violence is initiated by those who oppress, who exploit, who fail to recognized others as persons—not by those who are oppressed, exploited, and unrecognized" (p. 41).

And while Freire was a revolutionary, it was not one with the carrying of arms, but one that promoted education, consciousness-raising, and awareness. And for that he was forced into exile for his "subversive" work. Others were not quite that "lucky," resulting in the violent persecution of more than a thousand bishops, priests, and many laypeople, in cooperation with the CIA, were viciously threatened, disappeared, tortured, raped, exiled, and murdered in Latin America (Lernoux, 1980).

Among the countless known and unknown others, Archbishop Oscar Romero of San Salvador, El Salvador also paid the ultimate price when he was gunned down while saying Mass in 1980. Although, upon his appointment as archbishop in 1977, his fate would never have been predicted because, much to the dismay of the progressive clergy, he was the acceptable choice by the establishment. He was viewed as a conservative, not one apt to get involved with affairs of the state, and one who could disrupt the awakening of the religious, political, and educational consciousness of the masses (Sobrino, 1990; Erdozaín, 1981). However, because of what can only be considered a profound conversion, within three years of his bishopric, Romero was labeled as a subversive, incited violence, and was the greatest visible enemy of the rich and powerful (Brockman, 1989). Romero, who is a mesmeric image of Freire's notion of the prophetic church, responded to his critics with humble, but incisive remarks and action.

Romero's words and actions not only had (and still have) a sustaining impact on the people of El Salvador, but he also serves as a universal inspiration for all social justice workers.[16] In sum, Lernoux (1980) argues that the martyrdom of Archbishop Romero "… symbolizes the new alliance of Latin America's powerful Catholic Church with the impoverished masses" (p. xi). Indeed, Oscar Romero is a sterling exemplification of the meaning and intent of liberation theology.

FIVE CONCEPTS ASSOCIATED WITH LIBERATION THEOLOGY

To be concisely discussed below, there are five broad concepts that are identified with liberation theology: *Prayer and Biblical Dependence, Preferential Option for the Poor, Conscientization, Praxis*, and *Liberation*.

Prayer and biblical dependence. A dependence on Scripture, the following of Jesus, and a commitment to prayer is the place where liberation theology is rooted and emerges (Gutiérrez, 1990, 1984). As was in the case of Hélder Câmara and as in the case of Oscar Romero, both are exemplary illustrations of liberation theology and both make clear that prayer and union with God is where service to the people must have its foundation (Brockman, 1989; Romero, 1980; wLalli, 1999).

Pivotal to the prophets of the Old Testament, the four gospels, and the epistles are a chronicle of God leading His people to freedom from both external oppressive forces and internal psychological enslavement. The Exodus story is but one account depicting God acting on behalf of "slaves" and against oppressive rulers (Gutiérrez, 1973). Hence, a dependence on Scripture provides for liberation theology awareness and understanding of how God acted in the past, and that while entrance into the kingdom is the saving event, the kingdom of God is also present in the midst of the people.

Preferential option for the poor. The theme of "preferential option for the poor" suggests the willingness to authentically listen, work, and stand alongside the poor, as well as to share burdens and difficulties. Liberation theology cannot be discussed without realizing that the poor are central to the discourse, and moreover, as Boff and Boff (1986) assert, there are three levels of commitment to the poor: (a) visiting the poor; (b) scholarly research, writing, and teaching about the living conditions of the poor; and (c) permanently living among the poor.[17]

God possesses a "preferential option for the poor," not because they are necessarily better than others, but simply because they are poor and living in inhumane circumstances; it is in meaningful action toward our neighbor, particularly the poor that solidarity is intensified and we come in contact with the Lord (Gutiérrez, 1987). In providing further clarification, Brown (1993) makes the point that the notion of preferential option for the poor does not imply "exclusive" option, as if God did not love wealthy people; that would not be biblical.

There is, however, a tendency for some who are wealthy to be threatened by the notion of preferential option, seemingly placing them in a defensive posture. As Brown (1993) further elaborates, the poor, principally because of human greed, receive an unquestionable unfair portion of the world's goods, arguing "the fact that God does love *all* means that there must be food, shelter, jobs, and humane living conditions for all and not just for some ...So for the sake of *all*, and not just for the sake of some, 'a preferential option for the poor' provides a guideline for the kinds of change that are necessary to bring greater justice into an unjust world" (pp. 31–32).

In four of his encyclicals, Pope John Paul II asserts "that respect for basic human rights, especially for the poorest, is the litmus test of justice for a society" (Miller, 1996, p. 2). Finally, the pastoral letter from the National Conference of Catholic Bishops titled *Economic Justice for All* (1986) powerfully suggests that social and economic realities must be viewed from the perspective of the poor and powerless simply because it is a response to the biblical imperative to "love thy neighbor as thyself." The document goes on to assert that making a fundamental "option for the poor," is not only a call to consider the common good, but also so that the poor and marginalized are enabled in becoming active subjects in the civil society. Deprivation and powerlessness of those living in the shadows ultimately wounds the entire community.

Conscientization. As pointed out earlier, the educational theory of Freire (1994c, 1990c, 1985, 1975) had a tremendous impact on the formation, thinking, and praxis of liberation theology. The process of conscientization occurs whereby members of the indigenous community are given the opportunity and the freedom to evaluate their reality, which ultimately leads to growth and transformation.

Consequently, as knowing subjects as opposed to recipients and a move from a fatalistic perspective to one that is critically hopeful, individuals are able to deepen their awareness of their existential realities, providing for them a greater understanding as to how to change and transform those realities (Freire, 1985). Indeed, fostering a social reality where members of the community are critically involved cultivates a more hopeful and critical outlook toward ecclesiastical, political, and educational structures (see Chapter 5 in this text for a more detailed discussion on the concept of conscientization).

Praxis. Dulles (1977) suggests there is no separation between authentic prayer and action, which leads to what Gutiérrez (1984, 1990) would characterize as the intertwining of reflection on the word of God, leading to conversion and the word lived. Therefore, motivated by love and guided by faith, praxis is the interplay of reflection and action. This transformative activity leads individuals from a life of self–centeredness to a life of serving others (Gutiérrez, 1990).

Thus, liberation theologians see an integration, dialectical in nature, between the dimensions of faith and action. For liberation theology to operate, the interchange between theory and action is critical. If theory cannot be moved into action, the theory is lacking. As Cox (1988) asserts, "Theology guides action. Action refocuses theology. This continuous process of acting, reflection, then acting again—all in the light of faith—is 'liberation theology'" (p. 183).

Liberation. Liberation implies a conflict situation. As Gutiérrez (1973) asserts, "...*liberation* expresses the aspirations of oppressed peoples and social classes, emphasizing the conflictual aspect of the economic, social, and political process which puts them at odds with wealthy nations and oppressive classes" (p. 24). To put another way, the notion of liberation suggests that something or someone must be "pushed back" to bring attention to a problem, an unfairness, an injustice. Simultaneously, however, something must be proclaimed in bringing a solution or a way out of that problem or injustice.

95

Freire (1985) argues more clearly that in order to work toward liberation and move to a more utopian ideal requires a historic commitment to a pedagogy of denunciation and annunciation, further explaining,

> Denunciation of a dehumanizing situation today increasingly demands precise scientific understanding of that situation. Similarly, the annunciation of its transformation increasingly requires a theory of transforming action. Yet, neither act by itself implies the transformation of the denounced reality or the establishment of that which is announced. Rather, as a moment in a historical process, the announced reality is already present in the act of denunciation and annunciation. (Freire, 1985, p. 57)

Remarking on Freire's concept of denunciation/annunciation praxis, Gutiérrez (1988) underscores the point that this vision of utopia is grounded in reality, which is driven by action in the present–a historical dynamism, a cultural revolution–that works to subvert the established order in bringing about "…a new kind of humanity" (p. 137). In other words, for Freire, the notion of Utopia was not some "idealistic dream spun out of a mind ideologically enamored" (Goulet, 1973, p. xiii), but, rather, one with a very real possibility (Freire, 1996), and more to the point, one that is a "fundamental necessity for human beings" (Freire, 2007, p. 25).

And while structural liberation is critical, Gutiérrez (1990) also underscores the importance of internal psychological freedom and the liberation from sin. In the final analysis, sin is the reason for oppression and injustice, impacting values, relationships, and policies (Gutiérrez, 1973, 1990). Further making the point, Romero (1978) asserts, "Suffering will always be. It is a heritage of the first sin and a consequence of the other sins that God permits, even after the redemption. But the redemption converts them into power of salvation when suffering is done in union of faith, hope, and love with the Redeemer's divine suffering and cross" (p. 62).

Therefore, as Bonhoeffer (1959) argues, God's gift of freedom liberates one "…from every burden and oppression, from every anxiety and torture which afflicts the conscience" (p. 40). Most assuredly, thus, liberation suggests a structural, psychological, and spiritual new way of living in the saving action of God (Boff & Boff, 1984). Stated another way, "It [liberating praxis] requires personal transformation in self–awareness, a corresponding growth in freedom, and the creation of qualitatively new kinds of human relationships between men and women and between groups of people …Freedom is not a once–and–for–all achievement, but a lifelong process" (Schubeck, 1993, pp. 53–54).

IN SUMMARY

To understand the meaning, purpose, and importance of liberation theology, historical context is important. That is, the colonial heritage of Latin America and how it affects current conditions needs to be understood. Though, the parties involved are no longer called "Indians" and "conquerors," they are now called "the majority poor" and the "wealthy landowners" respectively. For example, in Brazil, 10 percent of the population owns 65 percent of the wealth, while the poorest 40 percent have just 12 percent. Indeed, Pope John Paul II condemned the huge gap between the rich and poor in Brazil (Simpson, 1997).

And more recently as earlier pointed out in endnote 5, Pope Francis denounced a "new colonialism" in which multinational corporations and global capitalism cultivate a system in which materialism is revered, inequality perpetuated, and exploitation of the poor is painfully evident (Yardley & Neuman, 2015). The sad reality, therefore, as Karlowich (1985) states, "...Latin America remains largely economically depressed, suffers from widespread social and economic inequality, extreme poverty, and authoritarian traditions; and continues under foreign economic control and political influence" (p. 21).

To that end, as long as these types of depressed economic, social, and cultural realities continue to exist, liberation theology will continue to remain relevant. Indeed, it is a theology that views history from the perspective of the marginalized and poor; that is, a "...history from the reverse side, the underside—the side of the poor" (Cleary, 1985, p. 86), or to state another way, liberation theology brings to history those who have historically found themselves "absent from the pages of history" (Gutiérrez, 2013b, p. 2). In other words, liberation theology views God as "acting in history," which suggests that faith corresponds to real historical circumstances.[18]

While the concept of liberation theology is rooted in the Hebrew Scriptures, underscored when Moses worked to set his people free, and is foundational in the Gospel message when Jesus first uttered the proclamation that He was bringing "good news to the poor and setting the captives free" (Luke 4), in a sense—paradoxically perhaps—liberation theology has gained a renewed attention, as evident by the prodding of Pope Francis. That is a good thing, for liberation theology possesses a powerful focus on what can be. In the final analysis, not only has Paulo Freire's work been instrumental in the forming and shaping of liberation theology, but it has been that same work that has had broad appeal in education, medical practice, political, social, and cultural movements around the world.

NOTES

[1]   Three days after his election, Pope Francis stood in the Paul VI Audience Hall in Rome to address the media, and explained the choosing of his papal name:

> At the election I had the archbishop emeritus of Sao Paulo next to me. He is also prefect emeritus of the Congregation for the Clergy, Cardinal Claudio Hummes [O.F.M.]: a dear, dear friend. When things were getting a little 'dangerous', he comforted me. And then, when the votes reached the two-thirds, there was the usual applause because the Pope had been elected. He hugged me and said: 'Do not forget the poor.' And that word stuck here [tapping his forehead]; the poor, the poor. Then, immediately in relation to the poor I thought of Francis of Assisi. Then I thought of war, while the voting continued, until all the votes [were counted]. And so the name came to my heart: Francis of Assisi. For me he is

the man of poverty, the man of peace, the man who loves and safeguards Creation. In this moment when our relationship with Creation is not so good—right?—He is the man who gives us this spirit of peace, the poor man … Oh, how I wish for a Church that is poor and for the poor! (para 7, Official Vatican Network)

[2] Actually uncomfortable with the term "father" of liberation theology, Gutiérrez, rather, sees himself as "nephew" (Allen, Jr, 2008). My conjecture of Gutiérrez seeing himself as "nephew" suggests a respectful nod to those who came before him on whom his inspiration and work rests, such as, among others, Bartolomé de Las Casas (c. 1484–1566). (For a detailed read on the life of Las Casas, see Gutiérrez's excellent book *Las Casas: In Search of the Poor of Jesus Christ* (1993)).

[3] It is no secret that under the papacy of John Paul II, with Cardinal Joseph Ratzinger (later Pope Benedict) as prefect of the Congregation of the Doctrine of the Faith, Gutiérrez's work had been marginalized, and even misunderstood by the Vatican, and though not officially silenced, he was not fully embraced. Other liberation theologians, however, such as the renowned Leonardo Boff, Jon Sobrino, and others, have been censured for their writings. Boff, a former Franciscan priest from Brazil was silenced for his inflammatory remarks about the institutional church and his alleged distortion of doctrine and Christological views, and Sobrino, a Jesuit priest, originally from Spain, but settled in El Salvador, was condemned for his writings in which he was accused of allegedly downplaying the divine nature of Jesus Christ.

[4] Reflecting on the significance of that encounter and the displeasure it especially provoked on conservative groups, Boff (2014) muses that that meeting was "…particularly intolerable to them that the pope received one of the initiators of the 'condemned' liberation theology…" (p. 118).

[5] Pope Francis commenced that change in atmosphere right from the start of his pontificate. In his first appearance to the world standing at the central balcony of St. Peter's, Francis did away with the gaudy papal cape as part of his dress, simply keeping with the white traditional vestments, adorned with the same cross he had always worn as both bishop and cardinal (Boff, 2014). Speaking to the people for the first time as pope, Francis in quick order asked the throngs to say the "Lord's Prayer" in unison, later humbly asking the crowd to pray for him. Moreover, instead of living in the Papal apartments in the Apostolic Palace, he opted to live in the Vatican guesthouse, enjoying the company of the community of bishops, priests, and visiting guests. These early simple decisions— but symbolically impactful—by the pontiff have come as no surprise to those who knew Jorge Mario Bergoglio; while as bishop in Buenos Aires he lived in a small apartment, cooked for himself, and took public transportation. Later, in Pope Francis' first trip outside of Rome, he sojourned to Lampedusa (a Mediterranean island) to greet and bring comfort to weary, hungry, and tired refugees making the treacherous journey from Africa who aimed to make their way to Europe for a better life (Cox, 2013). The release of his first Apostolic Exhortation, *Evangelii Gaudium* (The Joy of the Gospel) in November 2013 drew from the Vatican II document (*Gaudium et Spes)*, which underscored an emphasis on a care for the poor. In other words, in *Evangelii Gaudium*, Pope Francis not only revived the spirit and language of *Gaudium et Spes*, but the message of Medellín was also revived (Cox, 2013, para 5). Finally, as only one more example in which Pope Francis has been blowing a wind of changed atmosphere in the Church, he took a week-long, three-country trip to the South American Continent in July 2105. He first stopped in Ecuador where an admirer, Filiberto Rojos, fervently proclaimed, "We haven't had a pope like this in a long time, a humble pope, a pope of the poor, a pope of the people," and where in turn the Pontiff announced that we must extend "special attention to our most fragile brothers and the most vulnerable minorities, the debt that is still owed by Latin America" (Neuman, 2015, para 5, 17). Later in Bolivia he offered an historic apology on behalf of the Church for its role in exploitation, colonialism, and the grave sins that "… were committed against the native people of America in the name of God" (Yardley & Neuman, 2015, para 4). Francis also denounced a "new colonialism" in which multinational corporations and global capitalism cultivate a system in which materialism is revered, inequality perpetuated, and exploitation of the poor is painfully evident (Yardley & Neuman, 2015). The final leg of his trip took him to Paraguay, and while in the capital city of Asunción, he particularly wanted to visit the banks of the Río Paraguay to Norte Bañado, one of the poorest areas in the city. Constantly under the threat of being flooded, where shanty homes are made even worse by the elements, and where economic

deprivation is commonplace, Pope Francis shared with the people of Norte Bañado, "I have looked forward to being with you here today...I could not come to Paraguay without spending some time with you, here on your land" (de Diego, Flores, & Burke, 2015, para 2).

⁶ For the framing of this chapter, we looked to Kirylo's text, *Paulo Freire: The Man from Recife* (2011).

⁷ To say there is a "modern" emergence of liberation theology, of course, suggests that its theological perspective possesses an earlier beginning, which was one that came as a response to the European invasion to the "New World" in the late 1400s when the crusade of Spain and the mission of the Church became one and the same. That is, the establishment of a hierarchical feudal system of the mother country appeared to be successful, fostering a newly developed social order as a form of Christendom (Nunez, 1985; Dussel, 1981; Berryman, 1987). As a point of context, the concept of Christendom is attributed to the era of Constantine at the beginning of the 4th century, whereby Constantine, as an act of policy, united the secular state with the church (Muggeridge, 1980). Thus, as Dussel (1976) states, "Christianity is the Christian religion. 'Christendom' is a cultural reality. The former is a religion, the latter is a cultural totality which derives its basic orientation from Christianity...Christendom was not just an ecclesiastical unity; it was also a military and economic unity" (pp. 70–71). In that light, therefore, Latin American Christendom created ecclesiastical, cultural, economic, and political interdependence, which Nunez (1985) characterizes as "...an imposition of medieval, Spanish, and Roman Christianity, but not an evangelization that would convert people to New Testament Christianity" (p. 19). To be sure, the European invasion was the cause of the downfall and destruction of the Mayan, Aztec, and Inca civilizations. Within a year after the arrival of Cortes, the Aztec Empire was gone. Moreover, and though they lasted a little longer than the Aztecs, the Inca Empire fell at the hands of Pizzaro and his Spanish soldiers in three years (Van Doren, 1991). The Church was virtually silent about the death and destruction that occurred because they (the Church) "...sometimes doubted that the natives actually possessed souls, but never doubted that–in cases of resistance to the Catholic faith—death was better than life without Christ" (Smith, 1991, p. 12). These early actions by the Spanish and Portuguese established the beginnings for contemporary oppressive conditions in Latin America (Dussel, 1981; Gutiérrez, 1993). No longer called "Indians" and "conquerors," the parties involved are now called "the poor" and the "wealthy landowners." In that light, therefore, the thinking and action of liberation theology can be traced back to such religious leaders as Bartolome de Las Casas, Bishop of Chiapas (1544–1547), Antonio de Valdivieso, Bishop of Nicaragua (1544–1550), Cristobal de Pedraza, Bishop of Honduras (1545–1583), Pablo de Torres, Bishop of Panama (1547–1554), and Juan del Valle, Bishop of Popayan (1548–1560) who were among those who bitterly fought and preached against barbaric activities perpetrated by the Spanish and Portuguese colonizers (Dussel, 1981). Sullivan (1995) points out, "Indians had no standing as human beings in the eyes of the conquistador. Somebody had to become a voice for them, somebody who recognized their innocence, their human reality, and could awaken the conscience of the King of Spain and those who acted in the New World in the King's name" (p. 1). Among others, therefore, Bartolome de Las Casas became that voice and "... struggled for the integral freedom of the Indian not only in fact but also on the principle of their natural rights" (Dussel, 1981, p. 51). Las Casas' own rereading of Scripture and his reevaluation of his owning of slaves converted him to denounce the ill treatment of the native people, beginning with freeing his own slaves and becoming an unrelenting intercessor to local authorities on behalf of the Indians (Donovan, 1974). Las Casas' deep devotion for the rights and justice of the Indians stands as a profound example for contemporary liberation theologians. Brown (1980) states, "Instead of seeing the Indians as 'infidels,' Las Casas sees them as 'the poor' about whom the gospel speaks" (p. 23) (As mentioned in endnote 2, for a detailed read on the life of Las Casas, see Gutiérrez's work *Las Casas: In Search of the Poor of Jesus Christ* (1993). Gutiérrez, along with others, founded the Bartolomé de Las Casas Institute in 1974 in Lima, Peru. The principal focus of the institute is to work for justice, freedom, and human development on behalf of the poor and marginalized in Peru). These early acts of resistance to colonial Christendom were the forerunner of the present day liberation theology movement in the Church. Contemporary theologians look to the example of Bartolome de Las Casas, Antonio de Valdivieso, and others as individuals of active faith in the midst of oppression (Berryman, 1987).

⁸ For example, the following books represent only a few of the early works: Jose Bonino's (1975) *Doing Theology in a Revolutionary Situation,* Enrique Dussel's (1976) *History and the Theology of Liberation,*

99

Hugo Assmann's (1976) *Theology for a Nomad Church,* Juan Luis Segundo's (1976) *The Liberation of Theology,* Jon Sobrino's (1978) *Christology at the Crossroads,* Leonardo and Clodovis Boff's (1984) *Salvation and Liberation,* and Gustavo Gutiérrez's (1984) *We Drink from Our Own Wells.*

⁹ Regarding the notion of a "revolution" as a descriptor of a theology, Brown (1974) clarifies,

> The word [revolution] sounds threatening to those who stand to lose in any radical break with the *status quo,* but it sounds liberating to those who have nothing to lose but their lostness. Proponents of liberation theology insist that revolution need not be violent. They insist that the decision about violence will be made, not by the oppressed majority, but by the oppressing minority that has the power, the guns, the money, the influence. (p. 124)

¹⁰ Once again, turning to Brown (1990) who reminds us that through Bonhoeffer's struggles confronting the Nazi regime, he (Bonhoeffer) "…recognized that God cannot save us through domination but only through suffering with us, and this acknowledgment of the "weakness" of God made it possible for Bonhoeffer, who was 'a bourgeois of the bourgeois,' to grasp that fact that for himself as well, identification with such a God could only be achieved by identification with the lowly of this world with whom God had already identified" (p. 88).

¹¹ In providing contextual clarity and implications regarding the meaning of "*campesino,*" Erdozain (1981) states,

> …the dictionary equivalent in English is "peasant," but this is a word that hardly figures in the vocabulary of contemporary English–language speakers, and it conjures up a medieval, European image. The word "*campesino*" is cognate with campo, "field," "land." A *campesino* is someone who lives from the land, the fields; a landworker. In Latin America, poor *campesinos* own very little land and so are unable to support themselves and their families from their own holdings. They are thus totally dependent on nearby landowners, in one or another arrangement that almost invariably drives them deeper and deeper into deprivation, indebtedness, desperation, and readiness for change. (p. xxiii)

¹² It was, indeed, from these ecclesial foundation communities that liberation theology flowed. While literary credit is given to Catholic theologians and intellectuals, Brown (1980) argues that "The world's anonymous," the people are the real creators of liberation theology (p. 13).

¹³ Cámara (1971) passionately proclaimed, "Now the egoism of some privileged groups drives countless human beings into this sub–human condition, where they suffer restrictions, humiliations, injustices; without prospects, without hope, their condition is that of slaves [*sic*] " (p. 30). Cámara developed a lifelong friendship with Freire and was one who knew no fear when it came to challenging the establishment. Profoundly rooted in prayer and guided by the Gospel message, and even though he stood just over five feet tall and weighed approximately 120 pounds, he was viewed as a threat and an embarrassment for Brazil's military regime, and while he was subjected to countless interrogations and death threats, he refused personal protection citing the Father, Son, and Holy Spirit as his shelter (Kirylo, 2011; Lalli, 1999).

¹⁴ On his first armed excursion as a guerrilla, Torres was shot and killed by Colombian army bullets on February 15, 1966, in Patio Cemento in the department of Santander in Colombia, and Guevara, backed by CIA operatives, was captured by Bolivian special forces and executed on October 9, 1967, in an old mud schoolhouse in La Higuera, Bolivia. Remarking on his admiration for their revolutionary work, Freire (1990c) states,

> …Guevara's unmistakable style of narrating his and his comrades' experiences, of describing his contacts with the "poor, loyal" peasants in almost evangelical language, reveals this remarkable man's deep capacity for love and communication. Thence emerges the force of his ardent testimony to the work of another loving man: Camilo Torres, "the guerrilla priest." (p. 171)

¹⁵ For Guevara, love was a critical element in leadership, stating "Let me say, with the risk of appearing ridiculous, that the true revolutionary is guided by strong feelings of love. It is impossible to think

of an authentic revolutionary without this quality" (cited in McLaren, Che Guevara, Paulo Freire, & the Pedagogy of Revolution, 2000, p. 77).

[16] It is, therefore, no surprise that Pope Francis worked to have Romero beatified, which in the Roman Catholic Church is one step away from being declared a saint.

[17] Bonino (1975) strongly emphasizes:

> God in Christ identifies himself utterly with the man oppressed, destituted, and abandoned . . .We are called to this same identity in the double identification with the crucified Christ, and therefore with those with whom he himself was identified: the outcast, the oppressed, the poor, the forsaken, the sinners, the lost. This is the cradle of the Christian's identity and relevance. (pp. 145–146)

[18] In reiterating the point, Gutiérrez (1973) asserts,

> But the Word is not only a Word about God and *about* man: the Word is *made* man. If all that is human is illuminated by the Word, it is precisely because the Word reaches us through human history; Von Rad comments that "it is in history that God reveals the secret of his person." Human history, then, is the location of our encounter with him in Christ. (p. 189)

REFERENCES

Allen, Jr., J. L. (2008, October 30). Liberation theologian Gutiérrez says hope takes work. *National Catholic Reporter*. Retrieved from http://ncronline.org/news/liberation-theologian-guti%C3%A8rrez-says-hope-takes-work

Alves, R. A. (1969). *A theology of human hope*. Cleveland, OH: Corpus Books.

Assmann, H. (1976). *Theology for a nomad church*. Maryknoll, NY: Orbis Books.

Berryman, P. (1987). *Liberation theology: Essential facts about the revolutionary movement in Latin America and beyond*. Philadelphia, PA: Temple University Press.

Boff, C., & Boff, L. (1984). *Salvation and liberation: In search of a balance between faith and politics* (R. R. Barr, Trans.). Maryknoll, NY: Orbis Books.

Boff, L. (2011). The influence of Freire on scholars: A select list. In J. Kirylo (Ed.), *Paulo Freire: The man from recife* (pp. 235–269). New York, NY: Peter Lang.

Boff, L. (2014). *Francis of Rome and Francis of Assisi: A new springtime for the church*. Maryknoll, NY: Orbis Books.

Boff, L., & Boff, C. (1986). *Liberation theology: From dialogue to confrontation* (R. R. Barr, Trans.). San Francisco, CA: Harper & Row.

Bonhoeffer, D. (1959). *The cost of discipleship*. New York, NY: Macmillan.

Bonino, J. (1975). *Doing theology in a revolutionary situation*. Maryknoll, NY: Orbis Books.

Brockman, J. R., S. J. (1989). *Romero: A life*. Maryknoll, NY: Orbis Books.

Brown, R. M. (1974). *Is faith obsolete?* Philadelphia, PA: The Westminster Press.

Brown, R. M. (1980). *Gustavo Gutiérrez*. Atlanta, GA: John Knox Press.

Brown, R. M. (1990). *Gustavo Gutiérrez: An introduction to liberation theology*. Maryknoll, NY: Orbis Books.

Brown, R. M. (1993). *Liberation theology: An introductory guide*. Louisville, KY: Westminster/John Knox Press.

Camara, H. (1971). *Spiral of violence*. London, England: Sheed and Ward Stagbooks.

Cleary, E. L., O. P. (1985). *Crises and change: The church in Latin America today*. Maryknoll,

Cox, H. (1988). *The silencing of Leonardo Boff*. Oak Park, IL: Meyer–Stone Books.

Cox, H. (2013, December). Is Pope Francis the new champion of liberation theology? *The Nation*. Retrieved from http://www.thenation.com/article/pope-francis-new-champion-liberation-theology/

de Diego, J., Flores, R., & Burke, D. (2015). *Pope visits slum village in Paraguay*. Retrieved from http://www.cnn.com/2015/07/11/world/pope-francis-paraguay/

Donovan, B. M. (1974). Introduction. In B. de Las Casas (Ed.), *The devastation of the Indies: A brief account* (H. Briffault, Trans., pp. 1–25). Baltimore, MD: The Johns Hopkins University Press.

Dorr, D. (1983). *Option for the poor: A hundred years of Vatican social teaching*. Maryknoll, NY: Orbis Books. (Original work written 1474–1566)

Dorrien, G. J. (1990). *Reconstructing the common good: Theology and the social order*. Maryknoll, NY: Orbis Books.

Dulles, A., S. J. (1977). The meaning of faith considered in relationship to justice. In J. C. Haughey, S.J. (Ed.), *The faith that does justice: Examining the Christian sources for social change* (pp. 10–46). New York, NY: Paulist Press.

Dussel, E. (1976). *History and the theology of liberation, a Latin American perspective* (J. Drury, Trans.). Maryknoll, NY: Orbis Books.

Dussel, E. (1981). *A history of the church in Latin America: Colonialism to liberation (1492–1979)* (A. Neely, Trans.). Grand Rapids, MI: Eerdmans Publishing Company.

Erdozain, P. (1981). *Archbishop Romero: Martyr of Salvador*. Maryknoll, NY: Orbis Books.

Ferm, D. W. (1986). *Third world theologies: An introductory survey*. Maryknoll, NY: Orbis Books.

Freire, A. (1994). In notes of P. Freire, *Pedagogy of hope: Reliving pedagogy of the oppressed*. New York, NY: Continuum.

Freire, P. (1975). *Cultural action for freedom*. Cambridge, MA: Harvard Educational Review.

Freire, P. (1985). *The politics of education: Culture, power, and liberation*. New York, NY: Bergin & Garvey.

Freire, P. (1990). *Pedagogy of the oppressed*. New York, NY: Continuum.

Freire, P. (2007). *Daring to dream: Toward a pedagogy of the unfinished* (Organized and presented by Ana Maria Araújo Freire) (A. K. Oliveira, Trans.). Boulder, CO: Paradigm Publishers.

Gaudium et Spes. (1965). Retrieved from http://www.vatican.va/archive/hist_councils/ii_vatican_council/documents/vat-ii_const_19651207_gaudium-et-spes_en.html

Goulet, D. (1973). Introduction. In P. Freire (Ed.), *Education for critical consciousness*. New York, NY: Continuum.

Gremillion, J. (Ed.). (1976). *The gospel of peace and justice: Catholic social teaching since Pope John*. Maryknoll, NY: Orbis Books.

Gutiérrez, G. (1973). *A theology of liberation, history, politics, and salvation* (Sister C. Inda & J. Eagleson, Trans.). New York, NY: Orbis Books.

Gutiérrez, G. (1984). *We drink from our own wells* (M. O'Connell, Trans.). New York, NY: Orbis Books.

Gutiérrez, G. (1987). *On job, God–talk and the suffering of the innocent* (M. O'Connell, Trans.). New York, NY: Orbis Books.

Gutiérrez, G. (1988). *A theology of liberation, history, politics, and salvation* (Sister C. Inda & J. Eagleson, Trans., 15th Anniversary Edition). New York, NY: Orbis Books.

Gutiérrez, G. (1990). *The truth shall make you free* (M. O'Connell, Trans.). New York, NY: Orbis Books.

Gutiérrez, G. (1993). *Las Casas: In search of the poor of Jesus Christ* (R. Barr, Trans.). New York, NY: Orbis Books.

Gutiérrez, G. (2013a). The option for the poor arises from faith in Christ. In P. Farmer & G. Gutiérrez (Eds.), (edited by M. Griffin & J. W. Block), *In the Company of the Poor: Conversations with Dr. Paul Farmer and Fr. Gustavo Gutiérrez* (pp. 147–159). New York, NY: Orbis Books.

Gutiérrez, G. (2013b). Introduction (J. W. Block & M. Griffin). In M. Griffin & J. W. Block (Eds.), *In the company of the poor: Conversations with Dr. Paul Farmer and Fr. Gustavo Gutiérrez* (pp. 1–14). New York, NY: Orbis Books.

Gutiérrez, G. (2015). Where will the poor sleep? In G. Gutiérrez & G. L. Müller (Eds.), *On the side of the poor: The theology of liberation* (R. A. Krieg & J. B. Nickoloff, Trans., pp. 83–133). New York, NY: Orbis Books.

Haughey, S. J. (Ed.), *The faith that does justice: Examining the Christian sources for social change* (pp. 10–46). New York, NY: Paulist Press.

Hennelly, A. T., S. J. (Ed.). (1990). *Liberation theology: A documentary history*. New York, NY: Orbis Books.

Ieraci, L. (2015, April 27). Pope discusses literacy, dignity with widow of Paulo Freire. *Catholic News Service*. Retrieved from (Catholic News Herald) http://catholicnewsherald.com/features/vatican/195-news/roknewspager-vatican/7679-pope-discusses-literacy-dignity-with-widow-of-paulo-freire

Iglesia Descalza (2015). http://iglesiadescalza.blogspot.com/2015/06/the-meeting-between-pope-francis-and.html

Karlowich, R. A. (1985). *Rise up in anger: Latin America today.* New York, NY: Julian Messner Publishers.

Kirylo, J. D. (2011). *Paulo Freire: The man from recife.* New York, NY: Peter Lang.

Lalli, T., S. X. (1999). Dom Hélder Câmara: Poet, mystic, missionary. *Xaverian Mission Newsletter.* Retrieved from http://www.xaviermissionaries.org/M_Life/NL_Archives/99–N_Lett/BR_Helder_Camara.htm

Leo XIII. (1942). *On the condition of the working classes (Rerum Novarum).* Boston, MA: St. Paul Books & Media.

Lernoux, P. (1980). *Cry of the people.* New York, NY: Penguin Books.

Los Textos De Medellín Y El Proceso De Cambio En America Latina Primera Edicion (1977). (M. Hernandez–Lehmann, Trans.). San Salvador Centroamerica: UCA/Editores.

McLaren, P. (2000). *Che Guevara, Paulo Freire, and the pedagogy of revolution.* Lanham, MD: Rowman & Littlefield Publishers, Inc.

Miller, IHM, A. (1996, March). *Bread for the World in Louisiana, 14*(7).

Muggeridge, M. (1980). *The end of Christendom.* Grand Rapids, MI: William B. Eerdmans Publishing Company.

Müller, G. L. (2015). Liberating experience: A stimulus for European theology. In G. Gutiérrez & G. L. Müller (Eds.), *On the side of the poor: The theology of liberation* (R. A. Krieg & J. B. Nickoloff, Trans., pp. 11–31). New York, NY: Orbis Books.

National Conference of Catholic Bishops. (1986). *Economic justice for all: Pastoral letter on Catholic social teaching and the U.S. economy.* Washington, DC: United States Catholic Conference.

Neuman, W. (2015). Pope Francis lands in Ecuador to begin South America trip. *New York Times.* Retrieved from http://www.nytimes.com/2015/07/06/world/americas/francis-hailed-as-pope-of-the-people-arrives-in-ecuador-on-3-nation-tour.html?_r=1

Nunez, C., E. A. (1985). *Liberation theology* (P. Sywulka, Trans.). Chicago, IL: Moody Press.

O'Brien, D. J., & Shannon, T. S. (Eds.). (1977). *Renewing the earth: Catholic documents on peace, justice, and liberation.* New York, NY: Image Books.

Official Vatican Network. (2013, March 16). *Pope Francis: "Oh, how i wish for a church that is poor and for the poor!"* Retrieved from http://www.news.va/en/news/pope-francis-oh-how-i-wish-for-a-church-that-is-po; https://www.facebook.com/notes/vatican-news-agency/pope-francis-oh-how-i-wish-for-a-church-that-is-poor-and-for-the-poor/622559001093898/

Paul VI. (1967). *On the development of peoples (Populorum Progressio).* Boston, MA. St. Paul.

Planas, R. (1986). *Liberation theology: The political expression of religion.* Kansas City, MO: Sheed & Ward Publishing.

Pope Francis. *Crux: Covering All Things Catholic* Retrieved from http://www.cruxnow.com/church/2015/05/12/liberation-theology-founder-praises-new atmosphere-under-pope-francis/

Roberts, P. (2000). *Education, literacy, and humanization: Exploring the work of Paulo Freire.* Westport, CT: Bergin & Garvey.

Romero, O. (1978). In J. R. Brockman (Ed.), *The violence of love: The pastoral wisdom of Archbishop Oscar Romero* (pp. 1–242) (J. R. Brockman, S. J., Trans., p. 105). New York, NY: Harper & Row.

Romero, O. (1980). In J. R. Brockman (Ed.), *The violence of love: The pastoral wisdom of Archbishop Oscar Romero* (pp. 1–242) (J. R. Brockman, S. J., Trans., p. 236). New York, NY: Harper & Row.

San Martín, I. (2015, May 12). *Liberation theology founder praises new 'atmosphere' under Pope Francis.* Crux: Covering All Things Catholic. Retrieved from https://cruxnow.com/church/2015/05/12/liberation-theology-founder-praises-new-atmosphere-under-pope-francis/

Schubeck, T. L., S. J. (1993). *Liberation ethics: Sources, models, and norms.* Minneapolis, MN: Fortress Press.

Segundo, J. L. (1976). *The liberation of theology* (J. Drury, Trans.). New York, NY: Orbis Books.

Sigmund, P. E. (1988). The development of liberation theology: Continuity or change. In R. L. Rubenstein & J. K. Roth (Eds.), *The politics of Latin American liberation theology: The challenge to U.S. public policy* (pp. 21–47). Washington, DC: The Washington Institute Press.

Simpson, V. L. (Associated Press Writer). (1997, October 4). Pope decries Brazil's inequities. *The Times–Picayune,* A–26.

Smith, C. (1991). *The emergence of liberation theology.* Chicago, IL: The University of Chicago Press.

Sobrino, J. (1978). *Christology at the crossroads: A Latin American approach* (J. Drury, Trans.). Maryknoll, NY: Orbis Books.

Sobrino, J. (1990). *Archbishop Romero, memories and reflections* (R. Barr, Trans.). New York, NY: Orbis Books.

Sullivan, F. P., S.J. (1995). *Indian freedom: The cause of Bartolome De Las Casas, 1484–1566: A reader.* Kansas City, MO: Sheed & Ward.

Van Doren, C. (1991). *A history of knowledge.* New York, NY: Ballantine Books.

Yardley, J., & Neuman, W. (2015). In Bolivia, Pope Francis apologizes for Church's 'grave sins'. *New York Times.* Retrieved from http://www.nytimes.com/2015/07/10/world/americas/pope-francis-bolivia-catholic-church-apology.html?_r=0

EPILOGUE

A Call to Reinvent

In order to follow me it is essential not to follow me!

(Freire & Faundez, 1989, p. 30)

The implicit assumption driving the fundamental thought of this text presumes that at the core of what it is to be a human being is the recognition that we are ultimately spiritual beings. How people—be they religious, secularists, spiritualists, or naturists—live out or tap into that spirituality is, of course, varied widely and is dictated by human free will. Ultimately, the degree to which we individually examine, contemplate, or reflect on our spiritual lives is the degree that our spirituality is an influential factor on how we think, act, and work. Moreover, whether one is a doctor, mechanic, fast-food worker, educator, or whatever it is that we do, we bring that spirituality into every role and situation into our lives. The question, therefore, we all have to ask ourselves is how in tune are we with the spirituality that informs our lives and grounds our action? And why is that important? More later on those two respective questions.

As we reflect on the spirituality of Paulo Freire in this text, five broad themes emerge as we consider the implications or the "so what" for the critical pedagogue. First, while Freire was not one to proselytize, he was unapologetic about his love for Christ, making clear that that love was foundational in shaping his lens of the world, how he viewed himself, and engaged with the other. That is, this love for Christ was most visible in his obvious love for humanity. In order for him to comprehend the depth of that love with his neighbor, he took serious the notion of Buber's (1958) *I-thou* relationship. His love was not only authentic, but it also was infectious. What grounded that authenticity was a profound realization of the power of humility, and an embracement of the theological virtues of faith, hope, and love.

Second, through the prism of the theological virtues, Freire was one who deeply understood the dialectical interweaving of faith and action, one that particularly bent its arc toward the "least of these." Freire took seriously the Exodus story as a paradigm of liberation and the Lukan proclamation of bringing "good news to the poor and setting the captives free" (Luke 4:18), as the central call of his Christian faith. Clearly realizing the intertwining of the political nature of his work, he was always guided by four fundamental questions relative to the trajectory of policy, church, civic, social, or education decisions: In favor of whom? In favor of what? Against whom? Against what? (Freire, 2011). To be sure, Freire would echo Pope Francis' proclamation that one cannot reject the refugee and then call oneself a Christian.[1] Heralding the practice of the Beatitudes and yet unmistakably injecting his voice in the political firestorm of Mr. Trump's intolerant policies, the Pontiff exemplifies but one example that is rooted in those Freirean questions.

Third, Freire was a deeply perceptive man who was driven by an "epistemological curiosity" that invigorated him to connect with the world around him. He was continuously prompted by the question "why?" Juxtaposed with his deep faith and awareness of the Gospel message, he was well-read, drawing from a variety of perspectives in which his philosophy of life was shaped and his politics realized. Moreover, he formed friendships and collegial interactions from a variety of corners and diverse peoples, all of which encompassed a viewpoint that was saturated in the salve of celebrating diversity and that in that diversity we can find unity and strength.

Fourth, he was a man of indefatigable hope. Having endured imprisonment and 16 years of exile, Freire never relinquished his belief in utopia and the capacity for everyday human beings to move history in the direction of greater social justice and deeper respect for all human beings. He put it this way: "I am hopeful not out of stubbornness, but due to an existential imperative" (Freire, 2007, p. 26). Lack of hope was not an option for him. While he believed God provided the vision of that utopia, it was people organized around a common vision who made hope a reality. While history was always problematic, it also always remained pregnant with possibility (Freire, 2007).

Finally, though he became known around the world for his innovative educational philosophy and rubbed shoulders with political, educational and religious leaders across the globe, he always remained a humble man who enjoyed simple pleasures. He lived the Easter experience; he called people to embrace. He recognized his own unfinishedness and was committed to live and work in solidarity with the poor, the marginalized, and oppressed of the earth. Having experienced childhood poverty, he always sought one with the people throughout his life. As we have attempted to show in this volume, solidarity was not only a politcal stance, but a spiritual one as well.

In the end, it was not his politics that shaped his faith, but, rather, it was the foundation of faith that shaped his politics. This should be of no surprise because if one deeply uncovers the Gospel message, it is simply a message of liberation and justice, one of humanizing humanity. While Christian eschatological thought teaches that entrance into the Kingdom of God is ultimately the saving event, the Kingdom of God is also a very real presence among the people, working to set people free from oppressive forces—through the hands of such people as Freire and countless others.

A CALL TO REINVENT

To reiterate from the epigraph, to be a Freirean "follower" is to not follow him, but rather to "reinvent" him (Freire, 1997).[2] Paulo Freire was indeed deeply in touch with a faith position that informed his being on how he viewed and presented himself, how he engaged and treated others, and how he saw himself as subject in the world. In his own unique way, as suggested above—despite his flawed humanity-as in all of us—Freire became "Christ" on earth. Indeed, that is the call of all who claim to believe the Gospel message, to be the hands and feet of Christ. In other words, one does not necessarily need to say "I have good news or I am the good news" but, rather simply *be* the "good news."[3]

As per the two questions posed in the opening paragraph of this Epilogue, a more universal point is posited here. That is, regardless of one's faith position, Freire is of course not proselyting that we believe as he does; rather in that pathway to not following him and to reinventing him, he urges us to deeply examine our belief system and/or spirituality, the way we think, how we view the world, and what it is that individually grounds our lens of the world. And whatever that lens may be, it must be one that works to humanize humanity where all have a seat at the table. If that is not the case, then Freire would question whether that faith, spirituality, or belief system is one that comes from a space of love, faith, and hope. To state differently, the praxis of faith must always be one that works to diminish "the distance between what we say and what we do" (Freire, 1993, p. 22) in the effort to collaboratively lead all of us to be subjects of the world.

We are living in interesting times, volatile times. To be sure, Freire's thought and the undergirding of the type of faith he lived, the spirituality he illuminated and the theological perspective he embraced is quite relevant today, perhaps more than ever. In a current neoliberal climate where competition, privatization, and a system that inherently leaves some in and some out, and in a political climate that is dominated by a rhetoric of hate, separation, intolerance, and warmongering, it is quite evident that what is required is what Freire (2005) calls an "armed loved." This type of love is one that works to denounce injustice and hate in all its forms, and to announce the way of justice and liberation. As we see it, this begins with a pedagogy of resistance that works to speak up, speak out, and to be actively involved in the world around us in our commitment to humanizing humanity.

NOTES

[1]   http://usuncut.com/news/pope-francis-cannot-reject-refugees-call-christian/

[2]   Freire (1997) further elaborates:

> To reinvent Freire means to accept my proposal of viewing history as a possibility. Thus the so–called Freirean educator who refuses to reinvent me is simultaneously negating history as a possibility and looking for the teacher–proof certainty of technical applications... Reinvention requires of me that I recognize that the historical, political, cultural, and economic conditions of each context present new methodological and tactical requirements, so that it is always necessary to search for the actualization of the substantivity of ideas with every new situation. In other words, the way that I struggle against machismo in Northeast Brazil cannot be possibly the same way that one should fight against machismo in New York City. It may take a different form in terms of tactics and techniques, but it also has to remain true to the substantive idea of fighting against machismo as something unethical and undemocratic. That is what I mean by reinventing me. (pp. 310, 326)

³   To analogize consider the life and work of Mother Teresa through Thomas Moore's (1997) reflections written as part of the Foreword for Mother's Teresa's book, *No Greater Love*:

> Too often religion is imagined and lived as a purely spiritual activity, sometimes as a mental exercise in belief and explanation. In Mother Teresa's life and words we find religion's soul, in the sense that her faith is inseparable from her compassion, and her compassion is never disconnected from her behavior...What is absent in these passionate words [*No Greater Lover* book] of Mother Teresa is any attempt to convert us to her beliefs. She simply describes her strong faith and tells us about her work with the poor and the sick. Her stories are obviously not meant to convince us of her religious convictions; rather, they simply demonstrate how human beings, when given the most basic kinds of love and attention, find significant transformation and discover their humanity, dignity, and at least momentary happiness...Thinking of her as a saint, we might consider her example impossible for us to emulate...[yet] as she says, that we can all be saints—not without our imperfections and follies, not without our need to confess to failings daily, but nevertheless dedicated to the community of people, especially those in distress, who make up our family, our neighborhood, and our world. (pp. xii, xiii, xiv)

REFERENCES

Buber, M. (1958). *I and thou* (2nd ed.). New York, NY: Scribner.

Freire, A. (2011). *An interview with Ana Maria (Nita) Araújo Freire* (Transcribed and translated by J. D. Kirylo & A. A. Kirylo). In J. D. Kirylo (Ed.), *Paulo Freire: The man from recife* (pp. 271–289). New York, NY: Peter Lang.

Freire, P. (1993). *Pedagogy of the city*. New York, NY: Continuum.

Freire, P. (1997). A response. In P. Freire, J. W. Fraser, D. Macedo, T. McKinnon, & W. T. Stokes (Eds.), *Mentoring the mentor: A critical dialogue with Paulo Freire* (pp. 303–329). New York, NY: Peter Lang.

Freire, P. (2005). *Teachers as cultural workers: Letters to those who dare teach* (expanded edition). Boulder, CO: Westview Press.

Freire, P. (2007). *Daring to dream: Toward a pedagogy of the unfinished* (A. M. A. Freire & A. K. Oliveira, Eds.). Boulder, CO: Paradigm Publishers.

Freire, P., & Faundez, A. (1989). *Learning to question: A pedagogy of liberation*. New York, NY: Continuum.

Moore, T. (1997). Foreword. In B. Benenate & J. Durepos (Eds.), *Mother Teresa's no greater love* (pp. ix–xiv). New York, NY: MJF Books.

Printed in the United States
By Bookmasters